Praise for *Own the Change*

"An essential, must-read book for the sake of our youth and all of us."

—Bonnie Hearn Hill, KMPH-TV Great Day Book Club

"*Own the Change* is powerful. It brings to focus certain lost virtues: self-awareness, open dialogue, and the idea of investing in our youth. The book places clear accountability on adults and children to take ownership of their life outcomes. If half of Harper's vision is realized, the societal and economic changes could redefine the idea of inclusion in the USA."

—Ebenezer Ekuban, NFL (Dallas Cowboys, Denver Broncos, and Cleveland Browns)

"In *Own the Change*, Ralph Harper defines the continuing dichotomy of the United States: our professed values versus the ones realized and not realized for people color. Harper challenges each of us to step up for the sake of the next generation. The challenge is to release the shackles of our history and be personally accountable for the future. This is a book of hope based on realistic optimism and a pragmatic plan of action complemented with a sense of urgency."

—Robert Scott, VP

"It's forward thinking and positive. Ralph Harper's tactics to strengthen families and communities align with what researchers posit as a viable solution to improving deteriorating Black and brown communities. Imitation of empathy, love for others, and good behaviors should begin at home during early childhood. These qualities must be modeled at home so that children will emulate them in public. Healthy families yield healthy communities. We have work to do; but there's hope. More parents and youth advocates must light flames of passion for the future of our youth. It's the only way to get on track to make the 2060s decade a period of positive reflections. My hope for the next generation aligns with Ralph Harper's."

—Trillion Small, PhD, LMFT

OWN THE CHANGE

OWN THE CHANGE

How Our Children Will Lead the Next Cultural Movement

BROWN BOOKS
PUBLISHING GROUP

Own the Change
How Our Children Will Lead the Next Cultural Movement

Brown Books Publishing Group
16250 Knoll Trail Drive, Suite 205
Dallas, Texas 75248
www.BrownBooks.com
(972) 381-0009

A New Era in Publishing®

Publisher's Cataloging-In-Publication Data

Names: Harper, Ralph, 1961- author.
Title: Own the change : how our children will lead the
    next cultural movement / Ralph Harper.
Description: Dallas, Texas : Brown Books Publishing Group, [2019]
Identifiers: ISBN 9781612543291
Subjects: LCSH: Social movements--United States. | Americans--
    Conduct of life. | Political participation--United States. | Parent and
    child--United States. | National characteristics, American.
Classification: LCC HN65 .H37 2019 | DDC 303.4840973--dc23

ISBN 978-1-61254-329-1
LCCN 2019939667

Printed in the United States
10 9 8 7 6 5 4 3 2 1

Reprinted by arrangement with The Heirs to the Estate of Martin Luther King Jr., c/o Writers House as agent for the proprietor New York, NY.

Cover illustration by Tim O'Brien.

For more information or to contact the author,
please go to www.RalphHarper.com.

To Catherine L. Harper, my "mamma"—there are no words to stress my gratitude to you for prioritizing the lives of your ten children and others before yourself. You left us way too soon. Your profound passion for helping and guiding others has shaped me and brought me closer to God and His purpose for me. I will spend the rest of my life guiding children on a path of righteousness to the future—the 2060s.

To Black American children and the complete pool of underserved children in the United States of America and around the world: help accompanied by foundational guidance is on the way.

Erected in 1857 by the worn and scarred hands of slaves, Swayne Hall is the cornerstone of Talladega College. It's been a long row to hoe, yet the price still being paid is immeasurable. Spiritual symbolism marks the walls of Swayne Hall. The souls of many of our ancestors rest there. Slavery took its toll, yet Black Americans prevailed by clinging to a profound belief in possibilities—hope. May God bless the sacred land on which it stands, each structure that makes up its collective presence, and every student, faculty member, and executive that has and will traverse the realm of Talladega College for the purpose of higher learning. Talladega College: "the Alpha Lyrae Vega of them all."

Contents

Foreword   xi

Preface   xiii

Chapter 1: A Reckoning   1

Chapter 2: Perspectives: The Sixties   9

Chapter 3: If Oceans Could Talk   27

Chapter 4: Politics in the 2010s   37

Chapter 5: Hope   53

Chapter 6: Accountability: Tough Love for the Adults in the Room   69

Chapter 7: What It Takes to Win in the United States   87

Chapter 8: Workforce Development   101

Chapter 9: Workforce Development Life Principle: Reading   109

Chapter 10: Workforce Development Life Principle: Education   119

Chapter 11: Workforce Development Life Principle: Work   131

Chapter 12: Integrity   143

Chapter 13: Integrity Life Principle: Accountability   149

Chapter 14: Integrity Life Principle: Respect   165

Chapter 15: The Next Generation   177

Chapter 16: Next Generation Life Principle: Duty   185

Chapter 17: Next Generation Life Principle: Saving Money   195

Chapter 18: Efficacy: The 2060s Project Call to Action   205

Acknowledgments   219

About the Author   221

Foreword

My friend Ralph Harper and I pray everyone who reads this book has a deep burden to do something; to hear our children and not forget them; to see our children and not turn away; to support our children and "own the change."

In this magnificent writing, Ralph's words cry out to unite us around the greatest call of mankind—ownership and responsibility for our children's whole lives: their bodies, their minds, and their souls. We are, after all, responsible for following the principles and values of our Creator. Those values, throughout the globe, unequivocally and most assuredly require us to look after the innocent—the children of our land.

When Ralph and I first met, true to form, he was serving on a panel to share his experiences and solutions to address workforce disparity. The focus was on companies' responsibilities for diversity, equality, and inclusion. I was not surprised when he asked me to read a book he was working on related to Black American children and the next generation. Ralph suggested with confidence he had a plan to "change the world."

Ralph is a man of conviction. The kind of conviction to labor over every word while putting his work together. The kind of conviction to share with extraordinary transparency his own weaknesses, disappointments, and shortcomings. And the kind of conviction to lay it all on the line with straight talk, hard-hitting confrontations of societal dysfunction, and common-sense solutions.

Ralph shares his views about politics, fairness, and very real and relatable personal experiences—from race, bias, and discrimination to disappointments with his father; from shortfalls of his own to mountaintop experiences with his son and his career. Ralph has learned the hard way from each experience and bears it all. And while these experiences shaped him, they have not diminished him in any way. Ralph's will to steadfastly stay on his mission is unshakable. His conviction of ensuring a better and united nation is real. His goal is to make his priority our children and yours.

Coming from a conviction of my own about what leads to good citizenship and a fulfilling and successful life, I was more than intrigued. After all, the benefits of discipline, strong parenting, proper nutrition, a foundation of faith, education, and hard work—and their high correlation to good citizenship, economic success, and a fulfilling life—are no secret. However, it is also no secret that not all our children share in such a prophetic outcome or experience such a promising approach.

With great curiosity, as I read his work, I questioned—*What would my friend Ralph Harper do differently?* Why haven't we, as a caring, well-resourced, and prosperous nation, been able to solve these aged issues? Would I agree with his precepts? Could his plan catch fire? And then it dawned on me. No two people agree on everything completely.

This book is not about waiting for some perfect alignment of views on how we got here, who is most or least responsible, or debating some imperfect notion about a solution. This book is about the accountability of people. It is about being reliably dependable. It is about standing up and being counted. This book is about owning the change.

You will read it and get to know Ralph Harper well. Knowing him is a blessing. You will also discover an amazingly simple and straightforward model, the Ralph Harper WIN Model, which touts seven WIN principles—fundamental principles that are easy to agree with and support.

With each passing page and throughout each chapter you will see that common-sense solutions are closer than you think. You will see that you can make a difference with commitment. Be careful, though! Our current systems have left far too many behind, you just might hear the children asking, "Why haven't we changed before now?" You just might see the children as the hope and promise they represent for our future. You just might go to your mirror, look at yourself intently, and say, "For the sake of our children, I must own the change. Now!"

John C. Miller
CEO, Denny's Restaurants

Preface

Considering the genuine intentions of the founders of the United States, it is profoundly disheartening to witness polarization, discrimination, and inequality so prevalent in these modern times. And while the courage of a few with fierce determination to achieve our forefather's intended, righteous values has yielded measurable progress, our cultural norms have fallen short of the vision. In this era, when the entire United States population should be eagerly sharing congruent goals and working toward common worldly concerns like the preservation of our planet, our citizenry is still plagued by relentless divisiveness—a predicament that raises the questions: Why? What next?

Both Abraham Lincoln's and Martin Luther King Jr.'s lives were cut short way too soon. In each case, it seems, the work they started related to establishing the United States' foundational values was either significantly slowed or halted in the aftermath of their deaths. These slowdowns resulted from complacency and the willful capitulation of our citizens. Today, this level of inaction serves as the basis for the current polarized climate in which we find ourselves. For the last fifty years, I've witnessed racism, discrimination, inequality, and various degrees of calamity prevail. I've witnessed grown men, women, children, congressmen, senators, presidents, and people of all races simply stand down and drift into capitulation.

April 4, 2018—fifty years since Martin King was assassinated on that sad day. Sad because our nation is still running in place, fighting for the same social balance we once seemingly secured. And on that date of a significant milestone in United States history, we barely acknowledged (if at all) how King gave his life fighting for the future of a people and the future of our country. Here we are, more than 50 years since King's death and more than 150 years since Lincoln's death, fighting in different ways for the same freedom these iconic heroes once achieved. While it is arguable, we as a people in the United States of America have failed. We have done thousands of people who have paid the ultimate price to keep our values intact a disservice. So, as I teeter on the border of being accusatory, I'm compelled to admit my own guilt. No excuses here!

United States history and Black American history will always be tethered to the sixties decades. If for no other reason than that, we will commemorate key milestones achieved toward equality and the iconic figures who played roles in clearing those very important hurdles. As I reflect on the events-based continuum from the end of slavery, in simple terms, Abraham Lincoln laid the foundation for freeing the slaves in the 1860s, and Martin Luther King Jr. pressed on until voting rights and civil rights were achieved in the 1960s. Therefore, the freedom of all people in the United States was validated in the 1860s by the ratification of the Emancipation Proclamation. Furthermore, the equality of all people in the United States was validated in the 1960s when voting rights and civil rights were signed into law. So, as I thought about the situational and prevailing disparity in our country, it became abundantly clear to me that the single variable missing from the equation now is the accountability of the people of the United States to stand up and do their part in owning the change that has until now been evasive.

I have written *Own the Change* with purpose—the purpose of making monumental and measurable contributions to achieving the welcoming, free, equal values our country was founded upon. At some point on the journey to completing this book, I realized my purpose is aligned with God's purpose. Therefore, I am also committed for the sake of my spirituality.

For me, it was important to cover the pains of United States history. I believe many of our country's modern-day cultural flaws are linked to the outcomes of some of the United States' extraordinary conflicts (such as slavery, the end of it, a civil war, voting rights, and civil rights). Factions of our citizenry would have preferred the status quo or different outcomes. In this regard, because things did not turn out in their favor, they perceive some of our conflicts as unsettled. It's the kind of grudge that can only be resolved by our children over an extended period of time. This resolution will not happen in days, or weeks, or months, or a few years. Therefore, I made a very conscious decision to establish the end of the 2060s as the milestone date by which our country could be forever healed and cured from the self-inflicted scars of a turbulent past. January 1, 2019 to December 31, 2069 is exactly fifty years. My thought process was simple. Because it is apparent United States and Black American history will always be connected to the sixties decades, why not work toward a plan or a project to dictate positive outcomes in the next sixties decade that comes around—especially the life outcomes of our children? I have named the effort the 2060s Project.

It was also important to delineate certain key events on the continuum from slavery to the end of it, to the struggles and challenging efforts to achieve civil rights and voting rights, and up to the current point in time, at which our country has elected its first Black American president of the United States, Barack Obama. I put these events into context because with each of the major achievements toward Black American equality, there seems to have been a counterfaction-based response, including one that we are experiencing today in the year 2019—a response to there being a Black American president of our country. Large factions of our citizenry seem so consumed with that fact, they forget about the state of the most important demographic of our citizens: our children.

Most people of all races in our country were never taught as children what it takes to succeed in the United States. You know, those very basic and fundamental things required to survive and thrive in our country. I realized late in my life that no one ever gave me the precise answers or keys to success. Consumed by my personal experience with the audacity of racism, discrimination, and the history from which those ills were born, I learned the hard way. I was never taught to focus on a plan or prepare for the future. It is this reality that has compelled me to write *Own the Change*. Over the past several years, I've found value in telling snippets of my life's story and conflating these moments in time with meaningful action items purposefully outlined to ensure young children mitigate many of the pitfalls I experienced. I seek to give all our children the answers they need up front.

My plan's success will primarily be contingent on accountable parents, adults, and teenagers doing the right thing. Therefore, I will be banking on these three critical behavioral norms coming to fruition:

1. The hope of ordinary citizens of the United States and their belief that the required social and intellectual change I envision is possible.
2. The accountability of adults in our citizenry in terms of what they are willing to do to make our country better by appropriately guiding our children.
3. The will of our teenage children and adolescents to take the reins while guiding our country and carrying the burden of this heavily loaded agenda forward to the end of the 2060s and beyond.

Given these three contingencies, my focus will be on two distinct groups—parents and other adults with influence over children (such as mentors and teachers) and willing teenagers to take control of their life by engaging in and following the WIN Model REWARDS life principles that I will outline in this book.

At some point, every citizen in our country must realize and appreciate that they own a large part of their existence. Therefore, it matters what each person is willing to do to take advantage of the profound benefits of citizenship in the greatest and most powerful nation in the entire world, the United States of America.

After covering Black American and United States history, I will move into the modern-day place we've landed. From there, I will outline a strategy for parents and adults with influence over children and teens to encourage young minds in their quest to win in the United States. This is the goal.

The equation for success in the United is relatively simple. Once a person accepts that they are the master of their own destiny, they must strictly focus on developing certain skills that will allow them to legitimately earn money—ideally as a worker or as a capitalist. They must also keep their integrity in check as part of a plan to maintain their full rights to be free and positioned to succeed. Finally, citizens of our country must engage and do their part to support the next generation of children.

To guide parents and children with these critical tactics for success, I have developed the WIN Model, which includes three success categories: workforce development, integrity, and the next generation. Each category has certain life principles associated with it. I strongly suggest these seven

REWARDS life principles—reading, education, work, accountability, respect, duty, and saving—need to be instilled in our children starting with reading at three years old.

To be clear, I have written *Own the Change* for the benefit of all children, but I believe Black American children represent one of the most vulnerable factions of citizens in our country. Further, I have read a few books that suggest certain factions of Black Americans are still affected by the ills of slavery. The knowledge I have gained in this regard has polarized my beliefs on the subject into the affirmative. Yes, I believe my life on earth was affected by the ills of slavery passed down through my ancestors for generations.

Black American people represent the only citizen group that seems in many ways forced to live a very different brand of citizenship in the United States than any other race group. This theory is supported by real and readily available data points on discrimination, unemployment, income disparity, police brutality, incarceration rates, and more. Nonetheless, while these concerns are a Black American reality, these truths are not and can never be used as justification for unaccountability. Black American people must be responsible for their destiny. At the end of the day, being best in class will override the ills of a dark history passed down. Being best in class will transcend any special or unique brand of citizenship certain factions of our country may try to impose on Black American people. In the end, best-in-class Black American people will prevail and succeed in this great nation, which they can legitimately call their own.

So, while my views and bestowments of accountability in this book are at times biased toward Black Americans and Black American children, my greater vision is for the betterment of all children and the entire United States of America.

Now, let's go to work executing the 2060s Project! Who's in?

1

A Reckoning

The United States of America was founded based on a set of conceptual values that has never come to fruition. To get back on track to becoming the country intended by our forefathers, we must all, especially our children, understand from where we've come. Then, we must make conscious choices to go forward to the future, filling the cultural gaps that divide our citizenry so that the focus can be shifted to more constructive matters related to our existence here.

The Declaration of Independence, drafted by Thomas Jefferson, was adopted on July 4, 1776. It declared the separation of America from Great Britain and established three inalienable rights of Americans: rights to life, liberty, and the "pursuit" of happiness. The Constitution, adopted in 1787, established the initial framework for the structured governance of the United States and was intended to ensure the freedom of the country's citizenry. One of the most recognizable images in the entire world, the Statue of Liberty, was a gift from the people of France and dedicated to the United States on October 28, 1886. The profound message inscribed on the plaque inside Lady Liberty, which represents the "welcoming" values touted by the United States hundreds of years ago, reads:

> "Give me your tired, your poor,
> Your huddled masses yearning to breathe free,
> The wretched refuse of your teeming shore.
> Send these, the homeless, tempest-tossed to me,
> I lift my lamp beside the golden door!"

These and other United States milestones were achieved as slavery was in full force and Africans were a people enslaved. The values of United States laws and rights of its citizens did not initially apply to slaves. However, because of the will of a large faction of our country's people (abolitionists) determined to abandon slavery in the United States, the slow pace to the freedom of slaves persisted, and slaves were eventually freed.

In the mid-1800s, Abraham Lincoln became president of the United States. He firmly supported the notion of freeing slaves, and, in the end, slavery was the driving force for the Civil War. Coincidentally, both slavery and the Civil War ended in the same year, 1865, when the Union soldiers defeated the Confederate soldiers and slavery was abolished via the ratification of the Thirteenth Amendment to the United States Constitution. Nonetheless, these significant milestones were not achieved without a price. Also in 1865, Lincoln was assassinated before the Thirteenth Amendment was adopted as law.

Freed slaves became citizens of the United States in 1868 when the Fourteenth Amendment of the United States Constitution was ratified. But these varying levels of freedom—freedom from Great Britain, freedom of rights, and the freedom of slaves—ironically seemed to serve as the basis for the United States to continue to deviate from its forefathers' initial vision. Consequently, the dilution of perceived "inalienable" rights of (primarily) Black Americans, descendants of slaves, became and remains very apparent. Furthermore, it is broadly believed that separate brands of citizenship exist today for Black Americans and white Americans. Therefore, since the 1860s, a virtual tug-of-war has been sustained between our races related to differing perceptions of what is socially right and wrong with the United States. Although progress related to race relations has consistently overcome regression to the norms of those hopeless days of legal lynching, blatant segregation, and Jim Crow laws, the United States is, in many ways, still broken. In this regard, so long as all the people of the United States are not free and freedom here seems tiered—by race, gender, sexual orientation, religion, and other factors—the United States can never be the "perfect union." There's more work to be done—work clearly linked to the accountability of individual United States citizens.

Of the three fundamental rights of citizens touted in the Declaration of Independence, the right to pursue one's own happiness makes individual accountability clear. The Declaration of Independence does not guarantee a right to "happiness." It simply guarantees that all US citizens have the right to pursue happiness.

Since the birth of our nation, the people of the United States have proven time and time again that "happiness" in our country is based on two simple factors: what one is willing to do and where one is willing to do it.

Even when slaves risked their lives to escape slavery in the South, they did so knowing they would be free in the North. My decision to move from Birmingham, Alabama, to New York in the 1980s presented a different context of citizenship than my experience in the South. In short, I had better opportunities to succeed in New York City and Westchester County.

The irony of how the Democratic Party in the southern states supported slavery and the continuation of it prior to the Civil War while the Republican Party was determined to end slavery is daunting. Priorities related to the egregious ills spun from those dark centuries of superiority that are still being perpetuated today seem to have been completely turned around—one hundred and eighty degrees. The racism, discrimination, and inequality derived from slavery serve the purpose of sustaining the hopelessness embedded within the minds of factions of Black Americans.

Other than Black Americans, some large citizen groups seems scarred by the slavery experience, but in a different way. Evidenced by the fact that some of our citizens still believe in notions of superiority and race purity, the ills spun from slavery linger to this day. Some might suggest more so than the in-your-face legal race taunting of the 1960s. Some of our citizens count on "privilege" while failing to prepare themselves for success in our country. Consequently, far too many of our citizens are being robbed of their personal accountability. They have been slow to move on from our past—a real dilemma supported by the kind of subtle fray that lends to the sustained complacency that breeds inequality among the majority of our citizens of all races.

Accountability Is Powerful

Citizens of the United States are only as powerful as their will to do something meaningful and constructive. Far too many of our citizens live day to day while falling short of planning for the future. Too many of us make conscious—and in some cases unconscious—choices to yield to capitulation, sitting idly, waiting on our circumstances to change or for our perceived benefits of privilege to kick in. Content with leaving life to chance, some of us reduce ourselves to trusting the end result of existing casually with limited focus on the future, hoping this will suffice and yield positive life outcomes. Others take for granted the realities of existing in the United States, a country sometimes (more often than not) unforgiving. This problem is compounded when adults miss opportunities to ensure children are taught the importance of focusing, forward thinking, and garnering the will to be exceptional. Children count on adults for this level of guidance. Therefore, when adults fail in this very important accountability, our children fall short of envisioning and pursuing their full potential. If these norms of our culture do not change, adults are the ones who will forever be complicit in the continuous failure of our children and the entire country for generations to come. Today, the inaction of certain US citizens yields the predicaments we find ourselves in as illiteracy, lack of education, and disparity maintain a stronghold on our society.

My decision to write this book began with an epiphany I had about how the United States could be saved and established as the exceptional country its citizenry touts—a country more closely aligned with norms and values of its original creeds. Mindful of the fact it would be impossible to achieve such dramatic cultural changes over a short period of time, I reflected on the significant milestones achieved by Black Americans and others since the end of slavery—especially in the 1860s and 1960s. My reflections conflated with some of my modern-day cultural experiences—many of which have been starkly different than my existence in the South—inspired me to remain hopeful.

Hope has an uncanny way of engendering accountability and action in some of us. So, rather than just be consumed with hope about our country's future, I decided to write this book about how United States citizens could make a valiant attempt to dictate certain cultural and individual life outcomes in the future—over a fifty-year span and (logically) by the end of the 2060s. In my meditations, I imagined how the life outcomes of those citizens willing to engage and be accountable would be changed for the better. The financial and social impact of such a structured effort could be extraordinary—especially for Black Americans and others who are currently underserved. Imagine the success of unlikely individuals—especially Black Americans—enjoying the kind of prosperity and wealth exclusive to the upper echelons of society becoming common to minorities in the 2060s.

Nonetheless, my excitement about such a plan was interrupted as I also envisioned the profound undertaking required to yield the positive societal outcomes of the 2060s. The effort would be an arduous uphill undertaking. Much of what would be required would fall way out of my limited control— the commitment of US citizens, including President Obama and a plethora of other prominent figures from every ethnicity in the country; several decades of focus; hard work; the tests of the will of our children; and so much more. Although President Obama has publicly made commitments that he and First Lady Michelle Obama will be involved in the lives of our children for the rest of their lives, what will it take to convince them to appreciate my views and adopt my approach to a resolution for a persisting United States quagmire for which there is only one solution—the children of the United States?

In the next fifty years, our children will grow into adults. Some will be in their fifties by the time the 2060s rolls around. By not always focusing on our children in terms of feeding them the right values and making clear their accountabilities, our country is still on the treadmill of life—running in place. We are consumed with the same divisiveness from decades ago, which is sustained by aged norms and values completely counter to the values ratified by our forefathers. In this pivotal moment, the time has arrived to leverage our children for all the right reasons as we purposefully forge ahead with a clearly defined strategy: make the United States "great," in many ways for the first time. Nonetheless, because we have no other choice but for our children to lead this monumental undertaking, the adults are the ones who will be inextricably tasked with making sure our children are prepared for the long and challenging journey into the future. The adults in our country must selflessly guide and support our children in ways uncharted because our children will carry the weight of the future of the most powerful nation in the entire world on their shoulders into the 2060s. But first, we must have some appreciation of how and why we are in such a predicament. It began with slavery and the Civil War.

I firmly believe that the ills of slavery are with us today. The outcome of the Civil War haunts us as well—passed down for generations by whom? Children, through the teachings of their parents and other adults. Prejudicial cultural norms from the 1960s serve as the basis for our divides today—in many ways, intentionally implanted as wedges between the races. Yes, these historic cultural norms have been delivered to us through children who became adults. Ironically, the only good that can be derived from the phenomenon of perpetuation is a counterresponse of perpetuated goodness.

Just as the egregious norms of our past have been passed down for centuries, good and positive cultural norms can be imposed and passed down as replacements for the bad ones through the values of our children as they develop into adulthood. The only way to ensure US citizens reach the 2060s free of the strongholds of their self-inflicted calamity is with a plan to instill proper and fair core values within the minds of our young soldiers. Without exception, these values must include intellectual components related to our children's capacity to prosper. Therefore, we must develop our children for the workforce very early. In addition, our children will need to hone certain soft values—intrinsic qualities related to their integrity and notions of being accountable and doing what's right. They must also appreciate the value and importance of supporting the next generation of children. Furthermore, our children must be inspired to save money and become financially astute. In the process of instilling appropriate and meaningful values in them, we must be cognizant of the opportunity to develop them (on a broad scale), as best-in-class citizens must be at the forefront of this mission and journey forward.

Over the course of my life, I discovered the hard way that success in the United States primarily hinges on the will of people—what are you willing to do to WIN here? While the answer at a macro level is relatively simple; far too many of us don't think about it or focus on it enough. All it takes is:

- To be developed for the *workforce*
- Have sound *integrity*
- Support the *next generation* of children

Therefore, I created the following WIN Model, which has seven REWARDS life principles to follow as a guide.

The WIN Model

The WIN Model has three components and seven REWARDS life principles.

Workforce Development
- Reading very early in life (starting at age three) and on a regular basis
- Education as the absolute number-one priority
- Working and appreciating the value of working early in life

Integrity
- Accountability for one's choices
- Respect for one's self and others

Next Generation
- Duty—support for other children and people in need
- Saving money and being financially astute

Imagine millions of children from different backgrounds prepped for the future who make it to the 2060s in league with the best citizens our country has to offer. Our children's desire to WIN will have been tested. Moreover, the most powerful aspect of the solution will be evident as older children will have supported younger ones, and children of different races will have supported others who come from different backgrounds.

But for now, I bestow this profound challenge to change the United States (primarily) upon the shoulders of Black American children. It is my expectation that over the next fifty years, they *will* become best in class, as will be witnessed by their examples. In the process, Black American children will bring other children of all races along the journey to the 2060s. Yes— Black American children leading the way. Not because children of other races can't lead this quest. Black American children and Black Americans, in general, have a lot to prove. They will prove that being best in class will be the key to success in the United States. Being best in class will lessen the pains of our darkest days passed down for centuries. If for nothing else, Black Americans owe it to themselves to be united in the United States with focus on a single agenda and to be accountable to each other.

Moreover, Black Americans owe it to our ancestors who paid the ultimate price for the sake of our freedom. When we WIN, the souls of our Black American ancestors will smile down on us; freedom fighters of all races will not have died in vain; and the spirit of Dr. Martin Luther King will look down and smile on this great nation with pride. We may not hear his words; however, his strong oratorical voice will bellow out from around the world—the United States of America is "free at last."

2

Perspectives: The Sixties

Since the end of slavery in the 1860s and up to now, there have been eerie data points related to Black Americans achieving equality in the United States. While it seems no one was paying attention, every fifty years since slavery ended, crucial milestones have occurred. The parallels between both of the sixties decades (the 1860s and 1960s) are eerily behooving. In both those decades, exceptional citizens put their lives on the line for the sole purpose of preserving the cultural norms and values intended by our forefathers (including Abraham Lincoln, the more than two hundred thousand Union soldiers in the 1860s, Martin Luther King, the Kennedy brothers, and so many more freedom fighters in the 1960s). As a result, significant positive outcomes for Black Americans were yielded almost exactly fifty years after the sixties decades. Slavery was legitimately ended in our country in the 1860s, and voting rights, civil rights, and more for Black Americans were achieved in the 1960s. In what I refer to as the tens decades (1910s and 2010s), Black American citizens achieved major milestones that were directly linked to the freedoms provided from the 1860s and the 1960s. Fifty years after slavery ended in the 1860s, in the 1910s, freed slaves lived and thrived in a city called Greenwood, Oklahoma, founded by a Black American, O. W. Gurley. The success of this city of Black American citizens was so exceptional that the city became internationally known as Black Wall Street. Then, fifty years after the 1960s, in the 2010s, the citizens of the United States of America elected Barack Obama as the first Black American president of the United States.

Although this chapter is more about the 1960s, most of the commentary is about the 2060s and how Black Americans have an exceptional opportunity to lead the way, setting (on a broad scale) more examples like the ones Gurley, President Obama, and other Black Americans have set related to the positive outcomes of willful minds, bodies, and souls.

Black Americans' lives will always be connected to the tens and sixties decades. Nonetheless, because major change does not happen overnight, our children will be responsible for dictating the outcomes of the 2060s. Their success will be driven by an enhanced determination with appropriate will to ensure the trend of measurable Black American progress continues. However, Black Americans should not attempt to traverse the path to the 2060s alone, with just other Black Americans, the way segregation forced the citizens of Greenwood to do.

Because relationships matter, Black Americans should lead the way, working with anyone willing while setting examples for every citizen— especially the faction of our citizenry, of all races, whose lives are fraught with undue calamity.

After the abolishment of slavery, a new era for freed slaves was born—an era saturated with divisiveness, hatred, and doubt about the future of Black Americans. However, the future of Black Americans was also secured by hope of the enhanced futures of Black people in the United States. Because of the will of whites to ensure Blacks would not achieve equality, the long, arduous journey to freedom began. Far too many men, women, and children have been delivered to their senseless deaths in the process of achieving and protecting freedom for Black Americans in the United States. These individuals paid the ultimate price but never got to appreciate the profound value they added to Black Americans' existence in the United States—the kind of value which should never again be taken for granted.

The world will never understand the value added by very diverse and unique groups of people willing to fight to the death for the freedom and equality of Black American people. However, there is an opportunity for Black Americans to honor the strangers of many races who fought and gave their lives for the freedom of a people—Black people. To recognize them all by name would be a daunting undertaking. Nonetheless, we must always honor these brave and hopeful soldiers by keeping them in our prayers and by stepping up and delivering the kinds of successes that send very clear messages to the souls of the fallen and the citizens of the world—our freedom fighters have not died in vain. We must never again take their sacrifice for granted. I won't.

The 1860s

Black American freedom would not have happened had it not been for the courage, will, and tenacity of Abraham Lincoln.

Lincoln was born an ordinary American boy in Hardin County, Kentucky, on February 12, 1809, to Nancy Hanks Lincoln and Thomas Lincoln. His older sister, Sarah Lincoln, was born February 10, 1807. Conflicting stories surround Abraham Lincoln's younger brother, Thomas Lincoln Jr., suggesting he lived only three days and died in or around 1812.

Growing up, young Abe Lincoln was often at odds with his father. Nonetheless, he worked hard to support the family. Lincoln was a well-read, smart, and articulate young man. He soon developed into a crisp, compelling orator.

On the other hand, Lincoln's father was not always the one setting examples or conducting himself as head of the household. Typically, fathers are the ones who lead their children and teach them to step up and contribute to the well-being of themselves and the family. However, young Abe Lincoln was proactively taking the initiative and making sure he was accountable for making smart choices. He decided to prioritize working over achieving a formal education. His commitment to the family was unshakable.

On January 20th, 1828, Abraham Lincoln's older sister, Sarah, died while giving birth to her only child. Her death devastated Lincoln, as his sister (even though she was just two years older) had been forced into somewhat of a parenting role after the unexpected death of their mother from milk poisoning. Lincoln blamed Sarah's husband, Aaron Grigsby, for her death. He accused Grigsby of not getting his sister medical attention sooner. After Sarah's death, his relationship with her former husband, Grigsby, was at least tumultuous.

Lincoln started to dabble in politics when he was a young man, around the age of twenty-five. Due to his work schedule and his firm commitment to supporting and taking care of his family, he was left with no recourse but to read on a regular basis and educate himself. He taught himself law and studied fiercely for the bar examination. In 1836, he passed it.

The way Lincoln presented himself often won over the hearts of his friends and family members, who viewed his candor as fair and balanced. However, after he became a lawyer, Lincoln's candor, political views, and values earned him the nickname "Honest Abe."

Lincoln married his wife, Mary Todd, in 1842. As his life as a family man started to take its course, he experienced a series of unexplained misfortunes related to the untimely deaths of three of his children. His first son, Robert Todd Lincoln, was born August 1, 1843. Robert was the only one of Lincoln's boys to live through adolescence and into adulthood. His son Edward was born March 10, 1846, and died February 1, 1850; his son Willie was born December 1, 1850, and died February 20, 1862, and his son Thomas was born April 4, 1853, and died July 16, 1871.

After winning a few local elections, Lincoln was elected to the United States House of Representatives in 1846. By then, Lincoln had become very well known in the United States. However, his popularity in the southern states was not so strong. Lincoln had made his alignment with leaders in the northern states clear. He had also made his views against the expansion of slavery to new western states known.

In 1860, Lincoln won the Republican nomination for the United States presidency. He had run his campaign on a platform that involved the expansion of the United States into more territories or states, and he was adamantly opposed to the expansion of slavery in the new territories. In fact, as early as 1858, he had made his views regarding the notion of ending slavery broadly known. Although Lincoln supported ending slavery, he was clear in that he did not consider African slaves equal to whites, nor did he believe they should evolve to such a level of equality as a condition of the abolishment of slavery.

Lincoln was also against African slaves being allowed to vote or participate in the United States judicial process ("playing roles as jurors in criminal and civil court proceedings"). Nor did he support or believe in the "mixing of races by way of marriage." However, Lincoln believed "blacks had the right to improve their condition in society and to enjoy the fruits of their labor." Mr. Lincoln believed that "in this way they were equal to white men, and for this reason slavery was inherently unjust." Mr. Lincoln originally supported the notion of the colonization of slaves in other African countries and on nearby Caribbean Islands. He consistently stressed concern about slaves' ability to assimilate into US society/culture. Nevertheless, in the end, Lincoln abandoned the idea of colonization.

On November 6, 1860, Republican candidate Abraham Lincoln defeated Southern Democrat John C. Breckinridge, Democrat Stephen A. Douglas, and Constitutional Union candidate John Bell, winning the US presidency with 180 electoral votes. Lincoln won the election with just 39.82 percent of the popular vote. His victory was not the one the Democratic southern states' leadership was hoping for, and Southern Democratic leaders did not waste time with their snowball-effect response.

In December of 1860, in a direct reaction to the Lincoln victory, South Carolina became the first state to secede from the Union. Over the next year, several other states followed South Carolina's lead. In February of 1861, the Confederate States of America (CSA) was formed by seven southern states (South Carolina, Mississippi, Florida, Alabama, Georgia, Louisiana, and Texas) coalescing, with Jefferson Davis as president of the CSA.

With the news of the establishment of the Confederate States of America looming, Lincoln was sworn in as the sixteenth president of the United States on March 4, 1861. Just over one month later, the Civil War commenced on April 12, 1861 as Confederate forces attacked the South Carolina harbor. Two days later, Fort Sumter was taken over by the Confederate army, and the Civil War was initiated with Lincoln's response. That war would last for four long years and could not have happened at a worse time because Lincoln had been dealing with the deaths of his children—particularly his son Willie, who died in 1962 as the Civil War was in full force. Union army soldiers by far outnumbered the Confederate soldiers by an estimated two-to-one margin.

In the middle of the Civil War, in response to southern states that were unwilling to rejoin the Union, Lincoln introduced (signed) his first cut of the Emancipation Proclamation on January 1, 1863. This major initial step toward the complete abolishment of slavery was very limited in scope because only slaves involved in the civil conflict were impacted, and just a small fraction of the slaves were freed.

Frederick Douglass—"My Friend"

Later in the summer of 1863, Lincoln "unexpectedly" met a former slave. His name: Frederick Douglass. Freed by his own escape in 1838, Douglass had been openly critical of Lincoln's plan to free the slaves. Disappointed in Lincoln's slow pace, Douglass joined several other citizens and waited in line to meet with Lincoln on August 10, 1863. As he made his way up the stairs, he heard someone make a statement that seemingly referred to him and included the n-word. Douglass ignored the derogatory remark and went in to meet the president of the United States. Douglass had been recruiting Blacks to serve in the Union Army and had come primarily to persuade Lincoln to approve equal pay for them. The conversation between the two men was cordial, and Douglas was pleased that Lincoln treated him as an equal. In the end, Lincoln offered Douglas soft commitments that the Blacks serving in the army would be paid equally.

As the Civil War continued, Lincoln prepared for his campaign bid for a second term as president of the United States. He defeated Union general George B. McClellan and was reelected. On the day of his inauguration address, after his speech, he again met with Frederick Douglass in the White House. Although he was (at first) prevented from entering, word came from President Lincoln to let Douglass in. When he entered the room, Lincoln was waiting. "Here comes my friend Douglass."

On April 9, 1865, General Robert E. Lee, who had led the Confederate forces, surrendered to Ulysses S. Grant, and the American Civil War essentially ended. Close to 620,000 United States soldiers lost their lives (arguably) fighting for and against slavery.

A New Phase of Hell

Lincoln's executive order to free the slaves remained in effect until he was assassinated by John Wilkes Booth on April 14, 1865, in Ford's Theatre in Washington, DC. Lincoln was killed exactly thirty days after his last meeting with Frederick Douglass. President Andrew Johnson was sworn in to succeed Lincoln as the seventeenth president of the United States. After as many months passed, the Thirteenth Amendment to the United States Constitution, spearheaded by President Johnson, was ratified, and slavery in the United States was finally and permanently abolished on December 6, 1865.

In the immediate years after, a new phase of hell was ushered in for the freed slaves. As the very first Black Americans, they were essentially ignored by white Americans and the army in the South. Free with no means to survive, millions of Black Americans were neglected and left to starve to death. Previous slave owners offered to pay them to work. However, the gestures turned out to be trickery and a way to have the Black Americans returned to a new form of legalized slavery. An estimated one million freed Black Americans died from starvation and disease because of such neglect. Hundreds of thousands of the first Black Americans (freed slaves) were regarded as less than human by the same people of the nation who had benefited from their hard, free labor for almost 246 years. Imagine that. The mental and physical assaults imposed on Black Americans were somewhat balanced by the first federal law that protected the rights of Black American citizens—the Civil Rights Act of 1866. However, in December of 1865, southern white men formed the Ku Klux Klan (KKK) for the sole purpose of intimidating, terrorizing, and discouraging Black Americans from voting. Ultimately, the KKK's agenda was more far reaching than its original purpose.

That there were an estimated 260,000 Confederate soldier casualties in a fight to preserve the right to enslave a people is daunting. It is equally shocking that there were an estimated 360,000 casualties on the Union side of the war fighting to ensure the abolishment of slavery and the assurance that the United States of America would remain united and its values would prevail as a single country. Nonetheless, these obscene facts seem to serve as the basis for two diametrical beliefs or values surviving for all these years as factions of southern citizens cling to frustrations of defeat and other factions impose their will to move on from slavery and the Civil War in an effort to bring our country together the way it was intended. This dilemma contributes to the sustained race-related concerns that haunt our country today—racism, discrimination, disparity, police brutality, and consequently, separate brands of citizenship for Black Americans and white Americans. In this regard, the United States is still not "united." While our state geographies are mostly united by borders, far too many of our citizens are in many ways disconnected.

Some of my friends still question whether Abraham Lincoln was the one who (actually) freed the slaves. I imagine there is a large faction of Black Americans who cling to the same question. Although I accept Lincoln's view and the fact that he didn't support the notion that African slaves were equal to whites, the research suggests he was determined not to have slavery spread into new US territories in the West. Furthermore, he was the president who signed the initial executive order that started the process to end slavery in the United States. Beyond all that, Lincoln was, more than likely, assassinated for the role he played in freeing slaves—including engaging in the Civil War. Lincoln's initial executive order was carried forward as the Emancipation Proclamation—the Thirteenth Amendment to the Constitution. Moreover, Frederick Douglass got to hear Lincoln's firm commitment to freeing the slaves from his own mouth.

The facts are chilling each time I read or think about Douglass. Imagine: a slave who, through his courage, challenged his slave owner—the same slave who got into a fistfight with one of his many slave owners and beat him badly—a slave who escaped slavery—a former slave who taught himself to read—a former slave who became a business owner and a publisher—a former slave who (through the prism of many) was one of the most prolific orators in the United States—a former slave who became the most prominent Black American of his time—the same former slave who met with the sixteenth president of the United States of America, Abraham Lincoln, and more than likely inspired Lincoln and his successor, Andrew Johnson, to "do the right thing" sooner than may have been planned. Frederick Douglass no doubt encouraged President Lincoln to save a people whose free labor built the foundational basis for the United States of America and all its citizens, regardless of race, creed, color, or religion. Ultimately, Lincoln was willing to die for the sake of the complete abolishment of slavery in the United States.

The 1960s

After the end of slavery, and for almost exactly one hundred years, Black Americans continued to courageously fight for rights congruent to white Americans. The difference was that Black Americans were fighting for these rights as free citizens in what was now their country as much as it was white Americans'. Conversely, through a process of perpetuation, the norms of superiority had survived. While fighting for these basic rights, Black Americans were forced to exist under a separate set of pre–Civil War laws that had been enacted and reserved specifically for slaves who were now Black American citizens. These laws, labeled Jim Crow laws, were not just intended to ensure Black Americans would not achieve equal rights as white Americans; they were carefully crafted and enacted to extend the subservience of Black Americans. Jim Crow laws were the basis for white supremacy. The hundred-year fight—fraught with lawlessness—yielded thousands of casualties, as those white Americans willing to beat, lynch, and otherwise murder Black Americans were hardly ever punished or prosecuted for the crimes they committed.

In many ways, the horrifying and demeaning treatment of Black Americans by angry white Americans in this new era seemed to mirror the detriments of slavery. However, Black Americans would not be denied the freedom they had earned. As they continued their virtual marches and fights to the next sixties decade—the 1960s—they wore their courage on their sleeves with their will at the forefront of their presence. It was time to go to work—time to stand for something.

Prior to the end of slavery came the founding of Black American colleges. Former slaves William Savery and Thomas Tarrant founded my alma mater, Talladega College, in 1867. However, one of the best examples of Black Americans' will to thrive in the United States (despite social and economic headwinds related to effective segregation and Jim Crow laws) was the birth of Greenwood, Oklahoma. The town was confined to one square mile just north of Tulsa. Black Americans—doctors, lawyers, business owners—came in droves to be free and to build and run their own city.

At the peak of the migration, an estimated ten thousand or so Black Americans lived, worked, and thrived in Greenwood. They started their businesses and owned homes, banks, buildings, grocery stores, and a whole lot more. These Black Americans educated themselves and their children. They supported each other. They thrived in ways uncommon for Black Americans in those times (the 1910s), just forty-five years or so since slavery ended. Yes—they were sharp in their suits and hats and wing-tip shoes. But more important than these significant accomplishments was the fact that the Black American dollar circulated in Greenwood over nineteen times prior to reaching outside communities. Whites in neighboring communities referred to Greenwood as "Little Africa."

In the 1920s, Greenwood would become world renowned as the "Black Wall Street." Because of segregation, Black Wall Street was born. However, the strength of bonding made it impossible for segregation to serve as the catalyst for Black Americans to fail in their new homeland and their new town. Yes—in those times, Black Americans bonded and came together for the common cause of surviving. It was their only way—their only option. Then, on May 31, 1921, after a white woman accused a Black American man of assaulting her on an elevator, whites from neighboring communities went into Greenwood and, over a two- to three-day period, literally burned and bombed the entire town to the ground. Homes, churches, schools, and businesses were reduced to ashes. According to some estimates, three hundred residents were killed during the three-day riots. It is also estimated six thousand residents were under guard at the local fairgrounds.

As the will of Black Americans continued to swell, large factions of southern whites put on profound displays of resistance to any notions of equality. At the same time, with Jim Crow laws in full effect, hopelessness was settling in Black American communities.

Ground Zero of Racism

I can still recall the feelings of hopelessness when I was growing up in the South in the 1960s. I was born at ground zero of racism in Birmingham, Alabama, in 1961. At our peak, there were twelve of us living in a three-room house—my mother, my father, and ten children (eight boys and two girls). My parents were hardworking people who never seemed to make enough money to comfortably ensure the family would survive. On an as-needed basis, my mother would take several buses over the mountain to an affluent community, Mountain Brook, to clean houses. Determined to ensure her family survived each week, she worked to make a few extra dollars to make ends meet. Although the Jim Crow laws had all but dissipated, the power of these norms persisted. As I grew older, I witnessed grown Black men unwilling, reluctant, and, in some cases, afraid to look white men in the eyes. I could sense that hard work did not necessarily yield positive outcomes. My family, like many others, was consumed with hopelessness.

My family was constantly reminded that we were inferior and less than white people. We were reminded of these perceived realities by some of the absolute poorest white people in our neighborhood—people who were struggling with their own demons—leaning on the ills of slavery and lingering beliefs that they were better or superior for no reason other than the fact that they were white. Back then, it was normal for Black Americans to believe that regardless of what they did, success was not an option for their kind. This level of hopelessness was reinforced by the few shows on television with Black American casts—shows like *Good Times* and *Sanford and Son*.

These shows were closely aligned to the lives of Black American families in Birmingham. Each time James (the father in the *Good Times* sitcom) was close to finally landing a job, the opportunity failed to come to fruition. Fred Sanford, the junk dealer (Redd Foxx in a broken down pickup), and his son Lamont (in *Sanford and Son*) were always engaging in bogus schemes of trickery to make extra money. One common theme emerged. These families were poor, and they had no hope of moving out of the ghetto. That was all we experienced and all we witnessed on television. Like our neighbors, we were literally being conditioned into lives of hopelessness.

As a child living with my nine siblings and my parents in the three-room house in Ensley (Birmingham), Alabama, in the late sixties, I could sense there was something wrong with the way my mother and father were treated by random white people in our neighborhood. However, children were not always protected from the hatred in Ensley.

When I was around seven or eight years old, I went to Rosie's Store, which was less than a block away from our house, to spend my dime on some candy, a Baby Ruth. As I had previously done, I hung around the store, hoping the owners would offer me something else to eat or to play with—like a plastic ball or something. Bob, the husband of the owner's daughter, Anne, came into the store from the back door. He immediately jumped up on the icebox where they kept the sodas and started to install a blind over the window. Bob was struggling to keep the blind steady as he put the right end into the bracket on the right side and was trying to put the left end of the blind into the other bracket to the left. I noticed the cord from the blind had been caught on a nail, which was preventing Bob from lifting the left side of the blind to a height where it would fit into the bracket.

I yelled to Mr. Bob, "It's stuck." He ignored me the first time I attempted to help. Excited about knowing what the problem was, I yelled to him again, "It's stuck, Mr. Bob, the string is stuck."

To my surprise, Mr. Bob dropped the blind down to the icebox he was standing on, jumped off the icebox, and grabbed me by the shoulder of my tiny shirt. His eyes were bulged and starkly red. He started yelling rambling slurs of profanity at me before he took the cord from the blind, wrapped it around my neck, and commenced choking me. After several seconds, I was able to twist my way out of Mr. Bob's grip. I'm still haunted by the memory.

I ran home to tell my family, but in those days, they were helpless to do anything. So, my mother took a chance by calling the police. When the two white police officers arrived, they examined my neck and acknowledged the bruises. One of the officers suggested a few home remedies we could use to treat them before he and his partner returned to their patrol car and drove off. I imagined they laughed about the situation. They never went to the store to speak with Mr. Bob, the white man who, had I not escaped, may have killed me. My small story pales in comparison and represents a microcosm of the kinds of issues Martin Luther, John Lewis, and other civil rights leaders were determined to resolve in the South and in the United States.

Martin Luther King Jr.: "I'm Not Fearing Any Man"

Martin Luther King Jr. was born on January 15, 1929. His original name was Michael King until his father, Michael King Sr., changed both their names (when Michael was just six years old) to Martin Luther King Sr. and Jr. in honor of the great protestant reformer. His mother was Alberta Williams King. King also had two siblings, Alfred Daniel Williams King and Willie Christine King. After graduating from high school in 1944, King attended Morehouse College in Atlanta, Georgia. In 1953, King married Coretta Scott and earned his doctorate degree from Crozer Theological Seminary in 1955. The couple had four children, Martin Luther King III, Dexter Scott King, Yolanda King, and Bernice King.

King moved back to the South to become the pastor of a small Baptist church in Montgomery, Alabama. His move took place when racism was at its peak in Alabama—which was part of the reason King moved there in the first place. As most people know today, he became world renowned for his voice, oratorical speeches, and nonviolent approach to protesting inequality. King was hell-bent on seeking out opportunities to make the most egregious of situations right. His determination and his will to be the catalyst for change in the United States was unmatched. King's reign as the most prolific freedom fighter in the United States happened during some of the most turbulent times in the South. In many ways, the times were unsettled due to King's actions, which prompted responses from white Americans equally determined to counter his and African Americans' quest to equality.

The times leading to the 1960s were turbulent as well. But after the fights, murders, protests, and the end of segregation, signs of Black American freedom and equality started to surface in the 1950s. On May 17, 1954, the US Supreme Court, in the case of *Brown vs. Board of Education*, banned segregation in all public schools. On December 1, 1955, Rosa Parks inspired the bus boycott in Montgomery, Alabama, by refusing to conform to a law that required Black Americans to give up their seats on buses to any white person who did not have an open seat to sit in. Parks once said, "No, the only tired I was, was tired of giving in." After her actions inspired the bus boycott, Martin Luther King eventually took the lead. The successful boycott lasted approximately 381 days before bus segregation in Alabama was banned.

Martin Luther King founded the Southern Christian Leadership Conference in the early months of 1957—just as the sixties were about to roll in. Once again, the sixties would represent some of the most profound, successful milestones on the quest to Black American freedom and equality. Although King was not the only civil rights activist engaged in driving the agenda for Black American equality, his tenacity, sheer determination, and effectiveness combined with his powerful voice made him more relevant in the Black American community and, in a broader sense, the United States and around the world.

In the late 1950s and early 1960s, King staged several peaceful protests for Black American equality related to and against segregation. Many of the protests were confronted with violent responses from white citizens and state and local police. However, Black Americans forged onward with King leading the way with his nonviolent movements and strategies. One of his most notable, nonviolent marches was in my hometown, Birmingham, Alabama. It occurred in April of 1963, when I was just one and a half years old. King was leading a nonviolent protest with Ralph Abernathy when they were both arrested and taken to jail. King spent approximately ten days in jail for illegally protesting the treatment of Black Americans in Birmingham. During his confinement, he wrote a letter in freehand that justified his nonviolent approach to police brutality and the treatment of Black Americans. The letter was close to six thousand words long. Imagine writing six thousand words (freehand) for the sole purpose of getting your point across and making clear your will to fight and stand for something. That was who King was.

On June 11, 1963, Governor George Wallace stood in the doorway of the University of Alabama in defiance of President John F. Kennedy's order to allow African Americans to enroll at the university. The very next day, Medgar Evers, head of the local Mississippi NAACP, was shot and killed in the driveway of his home by Byron De La Beckwith. Evers's two children witnessed their father's murder.

On August 28, 1963, Martin Luther King delivered his "I Have a Dream" speech to an estimated 250,000 Black Americans, white Americans, and people of other races at the Lincoln Memorial in Washington, DC.

Less than one month after that speech, on September 15, 1963, when I was just two years old, four little girls—Addie Mae Collins, Cynthia Wesley, Carole Robertson, and Carol Denise McNair—were killed by a bomb detonated at the Sixteenth Street Baptist Church in Birmingham. The four Klansmen responsible for the deaths of these young and innocent children were Thomas Blanton Jr., Herman Cash, Robert Chambliss, and Bobby Cherry. Because of lawlessness in Alabama, fourteen years passed before the first of the four Klansmen, Chambliss, was tried and convicted of one of the murders in 1977. Klansman Cash died in 1994. He was never arrested or tried for the murders. Approximately thirty-eight years after the murders, Klansmen Blanton and Cherry were tried, convicted, and sentenced to life in prison.

On July 2, 1964, a poll tax that essentially prevented Black Americans from voting was banned by the signing of the Twenty-Fourth Amendment to the Constitution.

On the quest to achieve African American voting rights, Martin Luther King organized a march from Selma to Montgomery, Alabama, on March 7, 1965. The protesters were met by Alabama state troopers and some local police at the Edmund Pettus Bridge in Selma. After the protesters ignored the police's orders to turn back, the police attacked them with batons and released dogs on them.

The event was witnessed on international television. John Lewis, who currently serves in the US Congress representing Georgia's fifth congressional district, was beaten to near death as his skull was fractured. That day, March 7, 1965, became known as "Bloody Sunday." On March 21, 1965, the fifty-four-mile march organized by Martin Luther King and the SCLC was successful with federal protection. Five months later, on August 6, 1965, the Voting Rights Act was approved by Congress.

In the following excerpt from Dr. Martin Luther King Jr.'s speech, delivered to a group of Black American supporters on the evening of April 3, 1968, King seemed to predict the outcome of his own life.

And then I got into Memphis. And some began to say the threats, or talk about the threats that were out. What would happen to me from some of our sick white brothers? Well, I don't know what will happen now. We've got some difficult days ahead. But it really doesn't matter with me now, because I've been to the mountaintop.

And I don't mind.

Like anybody, I would like to live a long life. Longevity has its place. But I'm not concerned about that now. I just want to do God's will. And He's allowed me to go up to the mountain. And I've looked over. And I've seen the Promised Land. I may not get there with you. But I want you to know tonight, that we, as a people, will get to the Promised Land!

And so I'm happy, tonight.

I'm not worried about anything.

I'm not fearing any man!

Mine eyes have seen the glory of the coming of the Lord!

The very next day, April 4, 1968, King was assassinated as he stood talking to some of his friends and supporters on the second-floor balcony of the Lorraine Motel in Memphis, Tennessee. Seven days later, on April 11, President Lyndon Johnson signed into law the Civil Rights Act of 1968, which further enhanced the Civil Rights Act of 1964 and prohibited discrimination in housing based on race, religion, and national origin.

In November of 2007, more than 150 years since the end of slavery and 50 years since Black Americans achieved civil and suffrage rights in the United States, the people of the United States of America elected Barack Obama as their first Black American president. As the 2010s landed upon us, in November 2011, President Obama won his second bid for the presidency of the United States.

Albeit in different ways, the intangible scars passed down from slavery that impact certain white Americans and Black Americans are real. The plight of both races is evidence of a social and racial divide perpetuated for decades. But the norms of divisiveness and the horrors and conflicts born of it cannot and will not prevail.

Since the assassination of President Abraham Lincoln, twenty-seven male citizens have been sworn in to serve as president of the United States. Not one has offered a national and formal strategy or solution to the racial divides in the United States. The following represents the complete list of United States presidents since the Lincoln presidency:

17. Andrew Johnson (1865–1869)
18. Ulysses Simpson Grant (1869–1877)
19. Rutherford Birchard Hayes (1877–1881)
20. James Abram Garfield (1881)
21. Chester Alan Arthur (1881–1885)
22. Grover Cleveland (1885–1889)
23. Benjamin Harrison (1889–1893)
24. Grover Cleveland (1893–1897)
25. William McKinley (1897–1901)
26. Theodore Roosevelt (1901–1909)
27. William Howard Taft (1909–1913)
28. Woodrow Wilson (1913–1921)
29. Warren Gamaliel Harding (1921–1923)
30. Calvin Coolidge (1923–1929)
31. Herbert Clark Hoover (1929–1933)
32. Franklin Delano Roosevelt (1933–1945)
33. Harry S. Truman (1945–1953)
34. Dwight David Eisenhower (1953–1961)
35. John Fitzgerald Kennedy (1961–1963)
36. Lyndon Baines Johnson (1963–1969)
37. Richard Milhous Nixon (1969–1974)
38. Gerald Rudolph Ford (1974–1977)
39. James Earl Carter Jr. (1977–1981)
40. Ronald Wilson Reagan (1981–1989)
41. George Herbert Walker Bush (1989–1993)
42. William Jefferson Clinton (1993–2001)
43. George Walker Bush (2001–2009)
44. Barack Hussein Obama (2009–2017)
45. Donald John Trump (2017–Present)

Today we have choices—individual choices about the future of the United States. The question is which of us will yield to complacency, thereby holding onto the past, and which of us will be diligent in the process of dictating the future of our country through our children. Therefore, let me say again, the future of the United States of America—especially as it relates to race relations and the idea of eliminating our society of inequities—will hinge on the will and tenacity of our children. However, there are two very critical factors that must take the right shape:

1. The way and manner in which our children are shaped.
2. The will and determination of the next leader willing to shepherd our citizenry toward the next sixties decade—the 2060s.

I suggest that leader will be former president of the United States of America Barack Obama. President Obama could lead the way because he is a former president and the very first Black American president. He has the megaphone and earned media attention to efficiently spread the message across the nation. The president has a nonprofit organization, My Brother's Keeper, which focuses on a lot of what I will cover in this book. President Obama has said publicly, on occasion, he and Michelle will be focused on our children for the rest of their lives. For me, it's a logical choice. It will become a question of whether the president will formalize a national strategy to solve US issues.

3

If Oceans Could Talk

The American slave trade that occurred between 1619 and 1865 represents one of the most egregious acts in the history of mankind. Imagine the life experiences of slaves. These human beings were plucked from their African homeland like grapes from a vine, brought to America, and sold as commodities to be used as property for providing free labor in order to contribute to the construction of a nation—the United States of America. The visions of this reality are often too painful to bear. The notion that grown men and women were subservient captives boggles the minds of young children and adults in our country today. Babies born into slavery who lived their lives as children, adolescents, and adults in our country died the same way, as subservient slaves.

Visualize for a moment the unthinkable hell African slave captives endured on journeys from Africa to America—six-month stints across the Atlantic Ocean. Africans (human beings) physically and mentally subjected to forms of unimaginable abuse. Men and women reduced to subhumans as they lay shackled at the ankles, wrist, and necks in the lower decks of slave ships for weeks at a time with limited ability to move.

Their living quarters were filled with their bodies and darkness. African people stacked on top of each other as they waited—waited for the journey to end and the horrors of slavery to begin. These African men and women were rarely allowed breaks to relieve themselves. Infectious disease spread among them. Africans sickened to their core as they existed among dead bodies. These slave captives were beaten for no reason and sometimes for refusing to eat, as they preferred death by starvation to being enslaved. Many of the captives opted for suicide over the horrid conditions they were forced to live under. They took their own lives by abandoning the slave ships and drowning in the salt waters of the Atlantic Ocean. Their motionless bodies sank in a dreadful descent before landing on the ocean floor. If oceans could talk, the Atlantic would tell the stories of the estimated 2.2 million Africans who lost their lives on the Atlantic during the middle passage.

The slaves who successfully traversed the Atlantic and landed at the shores of America were not as lucky as the ones who perished on the Atlantic Ocean. Most of these slaves spent their entire lives forced to "willfully" support the foundational basis of America's expedited economic quest. They worked in the fields year round, in the depths of the cold and the elevation of brutal heat. Their shifts were simple—from sun up to sun down. Slaves were locked away at night and beaten mercilessly for making even the slightest attempt to learn the English alphabet so they could eventually learn the most fundamental basis for learning—reading. Whips cut through their skin and ripped flesh from within, exposing their bones. Imagine the pain. Grown men's spirits and their will to fight were literally and intentionally broken.

Young slave girls had no choice but to watch their mothers repeatedly raped. Slave mothers were forced to watch their daughters have sex with random strangers for breeding purposes. Women slaves watched their strong African men be reduced to nothing but bodies of flesh and bones. These slaves were helpless to retaliate—fearful of consequences guaranteed by any slight deviation from the order or process. Slaves were left with no recourse but to witness and experience (firsthand) the gruesome horrors of slavery—a lifestyle that became African slaves' cultural norm for decades, generations, and centuries. The inhumane treatment of slaves in the United States was deliberate and with unrelenting purposes. The average lifespan of a slave was just twenty-two years old.

There are conflicting stories regarding the American slave owners who, almost one hundred years after the first slaves were brought to America, invited William Lynch, a British slave owner, to America in 1712.

The American slave owners were interested in Lynch's tactics related to managing and controlling slaves in America, and Lynch was notoriously known for his aberrant ways of "breaking" them. Documents suggest the American slave owners met with Lynch several times at the bank of the James River in Virginia.

In Lynch's writings and speeches, he outlined, in graphic detail, methods for pitting young slaves against older ones, male slaves against female slaves, Black slaves against lighter-skinned ones, and so on. Lynch was confident in his delivery of a speech that outlined methods for managing slaves that aligned with similar techniques used to break horses. He often compared slaves to horses. Lynch described one of his slave management principles for economic planning as follows:

> Both horse and [n-words] are no good to the economy in the wild or natural state. Both must be broken and tied together for orderly production.

Lynch vividly described a process for breaking the "uncivilized" slaves as follows:

> Take the meanest and most restless [n-word], strip him of his clothes in front of the remaining male [n-words], the female and the infants, tar and feather him, tie each leg to a different horse faced in opposite directions, set him on fire and beat both horses to tear him apart in front of the remaining [n-words]. The next step is to take a bullwhip and beat the remaining [n-word] males to the point of death in front of the female and infant. Don't kill him, but put the fear of God in him.

Favored slaves were commanded to whip other slaves. The family structure of slaves was deliberately broken as boys and girls were sold off to other slave-owner families. Fathers were sold to other families as well—further ensuring the divide and strategic breakdown of the slaves' family structure. Lynch believed that these kinds of principles and methods of subservience and control would potentially impact slaves and their descendants "for 300 to 1000 years." Lynch was not alone in his thinking. I imagine the American slave owners did not invite Lynch to America just for talks and to have a few beers in Virginia. They became students of Lynch's teachings and applied his cruel and demented tactics, some of which are too grotesque to describe here, on slaves as the basis for maintaining control, superiority, and the assurance of inequality in the future.

Slavery in the United States was intended to serve two distinct purposes: the economic value of the accelerated development of a nation, and the assurance that white supremacy and inequality would prevail. Certain factions of whites were adamant that slaves and/or Black Americans would never achieve equality to whites. The will of white Americans to ensure the inequality of Black Americans has always been solidly grounded. It is one of the definitive reasons racial divides persist. Today, the same racism and racial hatred passed down from slavery is the reason the "United" States is still not united.

Could Lynch have been right? Are Black Americans still impacted by the ills of slavery today? Moreover, are white Americans somehow impacted by the ills of slavery as well? I think so.

In early December 2015, the United States' first Black American president of the United States, Barack Obama, formally commemorated 150 years since the end of slavery in this country. As part of the commemoration, Obama addressed the US Congress. During his speech, Obama displayed an unusual level of candor related to American history, specifically regarding slavery, civil rights, and inequality.

Obama recognized freed slaves who "risked their own freedoms for the freedom others." Close to tears, he went on to commemorate the slaves who "kept the flames of freedom burning with faith, dignity, and their songs." Referring to the Emancipation Proclamation and Thirteenth Amendment, he commended President Abraham Lincoln for his courage in the 1860s and the choice he made in "etching American values in our Constitution."

The president then moved forward one hundred years to recognize freedom fighters from the 1960s and before. Referring to the efforts and sacrifices of Martin Luther King Jr., John F. Kennedy, Robert F. Kennedy, and many others, Obama complimented the "moral force of nonviolence." He then recognized civil rights activists of the sixties and prior by suggesting

Americans "would do a disservice to our warriors of justice" if we were to "deny the scars of our nation's original sin still with us today." Obama's belief aligns with mine—the notion that slavery still has its grips on the United States of America.

For most of my life, I have believed Black Americans are and have been impacted by our ancestors' slavery. My personal experiences growing up in the South in some ways continue to validate my belief that slavery has affected my life. However, after reading the book *Post Traumatic Slave Syndrome* by Dr. Joy DeGruy, I have become convinced beyond doubt—more so than ever before—that my life and the lives of many Black Americans (many of whom will never admit it) have been impacted and shaped by the ills of slavery, as certain norms of slavery continue to this very day, passed down from generations ago. Dr. DeGruy has laid out her theories in a clear and concise analysis. It is a must-read.

A Punishment Passed Down

I was nine years old, growing up in Birmingham, Alabama. On a brisk, sunny Saturday morning, my close friend Bob Murray showed up at my house much earlier than normal—around 9:00 a.m. Soon after he arrived, we played with a rubber ball—throwing it back and forth for a short while as we made small talk. We decided to take a walk, one that turned into an extended, ill-advised tour of our neighborhood. There wasn't much to do; so, for the most part, we walked around our borderline desolate neighborhood, talking and coming up with silly lyrics for songs we hoped we'd get to perform as professional singers one day. We made a stop at our school playground, Councill Elementary. The concrete basketball courts had big potholes in them, which made them conducive for sprained ankles. The backboards were made of metal that had rusted over the years and had likely never been painted. The chain basketball nets on the goals were worn, and the strings of metal dangled from the round and rusty rim of the goal. The sliding board was wobbly and unsafe. So, we just decided to continue perusing the neighborhood, spending the little change we had on be-bops (frozen Kool-Aid) and junk food from the E-Zee store. We also stole ice cream sandwiches when the white owner wasn't looking—or had been turning a blind eye. He was the nicest white man in the neighborhood. Others weren't so nice. As we visited other friends' houses, we didn't pay much attention to the time until it was too late—3:30 or so in the afternoon. Both our parents were very strict; as we slowly walked toward our neighborhood, we silently anticipated the consequences of our mischief in our heads without commenting out loud about our inevitable punishments.

After we reached Bob's house, his mother, Mrs. Murray, immediately came outside on the porch to meet us. She screamed at us and cursed us on occasion—scolding and preaching about how worried people in our families and the neighborhood were about us. At times, Mrs. Murray spoke directly to me: "Ralph, you know better." She shared information I already knew. "Catherine is gonna beat your butt when she gets home." Mrs. Murray continued, "Yeah—I called her already."

I knew it was too early for my mother to be home from work. Reluctant to go directly home, I decided to follow Bob and his mother into their home. After we were all inside, Mrs. Murray continued with her chiding directed at Bob. Then she forcefully instructed him to take off his clothes. Bob immediately started crying. Meanwhile, I was a little confused about what was happening. As Bob continued crying, he was very slow to follow his mother's instructions. But Mrs. Murry insisted and became more forceful in her tone. "Boy—take off your clothes. I'm not gonna tell you again!" Bob finally took his shirt off so the top of his body was naked and completely exposed.

Mrs. Murray instructed Bob to lie across the coffee table. Bob's cries grew louder as the tears from his eyes flowed down his face like water from a faucet. He started begging his mother, "Please, Momma . . . I won't do it again." Bob was reluctant to lie across the table. Then, still confused, I felt a tear fall from my eye.

Mrs. Murray gave Bob what seemed to be a familiar stare before she instructed him for the last time, "Boy, you better lie across that table like I told you." Still crying and begging his mother, my friend slowly and reluctantly followed her instruction. He lay on his stomach across the coffee table with his knees touching the floor. Mrs. Murray, while still mumbling words under her breath, took a few steps toward the open door that led to the bedroom adjacent to the living room. She reached behind the door and retrieved a long brown extension cord that had been hanging on the doorknob. As Mrs. Murray returned to the living room, still cursing under her breath, she wrapped the extension cord around her right hand with her left hand. As Bob watched her every move, his cries grew even louder and into horrifying screams. Then the unthinkable happened—Mrs. Murray, a tall and mid- to heavy-sized woman, drew her arm back and (seemingly) with all her might whacked her son, Bob, on his naked back with the extension cord. The screams from Bob's mouth were unlike anything I had ever heard before in my life. I had never been so scared. As Mrs. Murray drew her arm back again to administer the second lash, I could not bear being there another minute to witness the brutal beating. With both my arms extended outward in front of me and both my hands at 90-degree angles, I ran several steps before I reached the Murrays' screen door. When my hands connected with that door, the force of my weight combined with me running as fast as I could caused the door to swing open 180 degrees before I heard it slam into the wall outside on the porch. I avoided the steps as I leapt off the Murray's porch and never looked back. I was running in full stride with my hands cutting through the wind like blades. My thumbs were pointed upward and straight to the sky. My head was slightly tilted back with my nose pointed upward at a 45-degree angle. As I ran, I felt I was running to save my own life. I just wanted to get home. I remember experiencing a sense of solace in my heart, knowing that my punishment would not be anything like what I had just witnessed at the Murray house.

Today, that experience—that imagery, those sounds of screams, the tears, the begging, the sound of that brown extension cord connecting with my friend's naked skin on his back from the force of a grown woman and that level of so-called "tough love"—serve as the foundation for my belief that remnants of slavery were passed down from the 1860s to the 1960s and may still be with us today. In my childhood, far too often, structured discipline, teachings, and planning for the future were substituted with beatings.

In 2014, the news broke about Adrian Peterson spanking his son with a tree branch that produced cuts on the child's backside, legs, and arms. I wasn't surprised. It was a form of punishment I was very familiar with.

It's the kind of punishment a lot of Black Americans—particularly those who lived in the South and other US geographies—were familiar with. In fact, many of us talk about it today. Mr. Peterson more than likely felt comfortable spanking his child with a tree branch because it was the kind of discipline his parents administered to him. In addition, it was—more than likely—what his parents' parents did to them and what his great-grandparents did to his grandparents. While it's hard to fathom, it is a reality. This form of punishment has been passed down generation after generation since slavery.

Today, the ills of slavery haunt both Black Americans and white Americans. However, the haunting is different for each racial group. I know because somewhere in the United States, a white father is teaching his son about supremacy by telling him he's better than others (particularly Black Americans) for no other reason than the fact that he is white. This is the way by which white supremacy and notions of superiority have survived for generations. I also know the ills of slavery are still with us today because there is a Black American mother or father somewhere within our borders punishing their son by beating him on his bare skin with a belt or an extension cord. The impact of slavery is still in our midst because Black males are still victims and vulnerable to a different form of slavery instituted via the US penal system. Black American men represent just 6 percent of the US population but 37 percent of people incarcerated in our country. I can feel the impact of slavery in the voice and tone of the Black American mother—so determined not to have her child adopt the norms of white people—as she scolds and questions her child for "sounding white" when her child simply speaks English properly. The determination to ensure the inequality of Black Americans from the slave era is still in force today when the men and women sworn in to protect and serve the citizenry are comfortable shooting unarmed Black American men—sometimes in the back, killing them—because the chances that there will be no consequences for their actions weigh heavily in their favor. Black Americans' lives are fraught with the ills of slavery because the same hopelessness passed down for more than 150 years seems to rob them of their accountability and will to properly guide their children in ways that will increase their chances at making it in the United States. These are the kinds of norms that haunt Black and white Americans. These are the habits that must be eradicated.

In 1978, George Benson released "The Greatest Love of All." In this song, Benson featured children as society's number-one priority. He explained how the children of the world represent the future. Benson talked about children leading as they grow into adulthood. He reminded adults about the need and accountability we have to "teach our children well." He made clear the opportunity adults have to make life easier for children while suggesting our children should not be forced to experience the exact same pitfalls as their parents.

Unlike the discussions led by adults in the room that ultimately yielded an outcome that ended Apartheid in South Africa, the future of the United States hinges on the values and will brought up with the children. We must accept this reality, as the future of our country will heavily depend on the way adults comport themselves in support of our children. The values we instill within them today will serve as the foundation of their beliefs and their will to make the right choices as they grow up to lead the United States to a very different place. If you are an adult citizen of the United States, you have a responsibility to get this right. It is up to you to shape and reshape our children in ways that make them comfortable leaving a dark past behind on a quest toward a brighter future by the 2060s.

4

Politics in the 2010s

The US population is more diverse now than ever before. Over the next decade or so, the diversity could get much better or worse depending on which side of the aisle your vision or views lie. The estimated breakdown of the population by race is as follows: 72 percent white (including Hispanic), 13 percent Black, 5 percent Asian, 0.9 percent American Indian, 0.1 percent Native Hawaiian, 3 percent mixed, and 6 percent other. While the United States has made significant strides in terms of race relations, it is very apparent there is more work to be done. The scars imposed upon our country that derived from slavery, the Civil War, and the racial divides that ensued are oftentimes more prevalent than one would think they should be after so many years since the 1860s. These scars of division are still firmly planted in our modern-day culture, seemingly hiding in plain sight.

Ironically, in this decade (the 2010s), several factions of US citizens commemorated significant milestones of the 1860s, the 1910s, and the 1960s. It's been 150 years since slavery ended; 100 years since Black Wall Street was thriving; and 50 years since the events of the 1960s and the fights for civil and voting rights. But here we are in the 2010s, and—like clockwork—50 years later, another significant milestone was achieved related to Black Americans' journey to equality: Barack Obama was elected president of the United States.

The end of slavery and each of the milestones that have followed somehow yielded significant and notably positive outcomes that seemed to align with our forefathers' visions and their intended values for the United States. However, each success has been followed by a very negative national response.

- The response to the end of slavery in 1865 was the intentional starvation and lynching of over one million freed slaves.
- The response to Black Wall Street, the town founded by Black Americans that thrived in the 1910s, was the burning and bombing of the city after a white girl accused a young Black American man of touching or flirting with her. Several Black Americans lost their lives while others were incarcerated for years. Black Wall Street never recovered, and there has been nothing like it since.
- The response to the achievement of voting rights, civil rights, and so much more in the 1960s was the assassinations of Bobby Kennedy, John F. Kennedy, Martin Luther King, and four little girls (Black American children) who were senselessly bombed at Sixteenth Street Baptist Church in my hometown of Birmingham, Alabama, as well as the brutal beating of future congressman John Lewis and several more deaths of freedom fighters.
- The response to Barack Obama, the first Black American president of the United States of America, is being witnessed now as I write this paragraph. Militia groups increased by close to 1000 percent after Obama was elected to his second term. Police brutality increased as random police applied deadly force upon several Black American men and boys during the Obama presidency; Dylann Roof killed (in cold blood) nine Black Americans at a South Carolina church; the US Congress has responded with its unique brands of actions and inactions against President Obama; our citizenry has legitimately delivered Donald Trump to the presidency, and some believe the Klan is being emboldened and sponsored by our current president, Donald Trump.

Barack Obama and New Hope

The 2010s has not just been about our history. This decade has yielded something that had always been hard to even imagine—a young Black

American man with a "funny name," Barack Obama, becoming president of the United States. I had never heard of him when he initially came on the scene. However, over a short period of time, Barack Obama moved quickly from serving as a community organizer to becoming an Illinois state senator, to becoming a candidate for the US Senate seat representing the state of Illinois, to becoming selected as the person to deliver the keynote speech at the Democratic Convention, to winning his bid for the US Senate, to becoming the Democratic candidate for president of the United States, to actually being elected the first Black or African American president of the United States of America.

While running for the Senate, Obama was selected to deliver the keynote speech at the 2004 Democratic National Convention (DNC). He was virtually unknown at the time, and it must have been a little perplexing for many US citizens as to why he had been tapped. It was as if he had come out of nowhere, standing on stage, addressing thousands of Democrats—inspiring them to vote. However, in that moment, in his brief timeslot on the world stage, he stole the show. Obama began his speech by tracing his family from Kenya to the United States and Hawaii. He talked about his and his family's plight and then balanced the message with his father's and his family's strong will to be educated. His most rousing deliveries came when he spoke of hope for the United States. It is virtually impossible to address the United States without addressing race. Obama put race into context by suggesting, "There's not a Black America and white America and Latino America and Asian America; there's the United States of America." Again, the crowd was literally standing and shouting among deafening applause. It was one of the most powerful speeches delivered in the United States about the hope for the future of our country. It was the kind of speech that needed to be delivered and heard more often. In the end, Obama completed his DNC speech by throwing full support behind John Kerry and John Edwards for the offices of president and vice president of the United States.

Obama's speech and performance at the DNC in 2004 turned out to be more profound than most of us knew. The strategy had worked; his popularity grew. He won his US Senate race and became one of the two senators for the state of Illinois. Moreover, there seemed to be a sea swell occurring related to Democrats garnering higher levels of fuel and appetite for change and hope—the same change and hope Obama touted and advocated for in his book *The Audacity of Hope*. The excitement in Black American communities was especially noticeable. Furthermore, there was a sense of growing optimism that reached far beyond Black American communities—optimism in anticipation of the 2010s as rumors started to spread about an Obama candidacy in the 2008 presidential election. Then it happened. Two years into his obligation as US senator from the state of Illinois, Barack Obama was scheduled to deliver his presidential bid announcement speech. He would deliver the speech at the old state capitol in Illinois, the same venue where Abraham Lincoln, our sixteenth president—the same US president who won his bid for presidency and made his priority ending slavery—had started his political career.

There he was, on February 10, 2007, the young Harvard graduate literally standing in the faded footprints of President Lincoln, delivering yet another rousing speech: his announcement that he would run for the office of president of the United States in the 2008 election.

Black Americans (men and women) had previously campaigned and run for the highest office in the United State. Frederick Douglass was the first, in 1848; then Shirley Chisholm in 1972, Jesse Jackson in 1984 and 1988, Alan Keyes in 1996, 2000, and 2008, Al Sharpton in 2004, Herman Cain in 2012, and a significant number of others. However, this candidacy felt different to me—very different. The speech Obama had delivered at the DNC in 2004 had inspired millions of citizens of the United States—citizens of many races. Black Americans were especially eager to throw support behind candidate Obama. However, the number of white Americans wearing their support for Obama on their sleeves was astonishing. There was a strong sense of hopeful energy that consumed the social atmosphere and the political climate in different and vast geographies of the United States. The newfound hope in the country caused ordinary people to anticipate a new beginning in the United States. For me, it felt like a new era had arrived, accompanied by an extraordinary potential to cause our country to finally live up to its welcoming creed and values of acceptance. There was hope that, this time, Black Americans would get to experience (for the first time) the best the United States had to offer in reconciliation since slavery.

As in previous elections when Black Americans had run for president, the initial response to Obama's decision was met with mixed emotions and premature doubt regarding his chances of winning. However, his speeches, his tone, his style, his good looks, his message, and his hope and optimism started to resonate with Democrats. His determination and his messages, couched in language about the future of our country, our children, and a truly united United States of America, caused a storm to brew. It was an outcome only Barack Obama and his wife, Michelle Obama, anticipated. Day by day, week by week, month by month, his crowds in major and small cities around the country grew bigger—and, in some cases, uncontrolled and tainted with protests, even death threats. The tumult was almost uncontrollable, leaving Obama with no recourse but to request Secret Service protection earlier than any other previous presidential candidate. It was clear not everybody was excited about the possibility that a Black American man could actually become president of the United States.

As Obama's candidacy moved deeper into full swing, the energy he had fueled started to spark interest beyond US borders. Europeans and their leaders started to show support for Obama. The world was becoming energized by Obama's visions. His messages crossed the circumference of the entire globe, resonating with citizens of the entire world, who, mindful of a polarized United States, placed hopeful thoughts on the possibility that the country would leverage Obama's unmatched optimism, and somehow our country's people would be forever united, thus ensuring the country's original founding principles would finally come to fruition. Again, Black Americans seemed more hopeful than ever before. Conversely, those citizens who by now had started to make their disdain for a possible Obama presidency more pronounced started to freely present their views in public. Nonetheless, Obama's will and his support had grown way too strong—out of control and, some might have suggested, out of his hands. The strength of his candidacy was firmly validated when, on his way to visit Germany, he crossed the Atlantic, where over 2.2 million Africans lost their lives during the Middle Passage. In Germany, Obama was greeted by an estimated two hundred thousand German citizens.

You may recall, on the campaign trail, the woman in red at the McCain rally who accepted the mic from John McCain to make a comment. To arouse the group of McCain supporters, she said hesitantly, "I can't trust Obama . . . I have read about him and . . . he's"—she paused—"an Arab."

Shaking his head in disagreement, McCain immediately retrieved the mic from the woman and started to respond. McCain said, "No . . . No," as boos from the audience in response to him shaking his head in disagreement grew louder. As the few supporters in the crowd started to boo McCain more aggressively, the woman in disbelief reacted to McCain with a question: "He's not?"

McCain continued, "No! He's a decent family man—citizen—who I just happen to have disagreements with."

Some of McCain's audience could be heard continuing to boo McCain's response. Unfazed, McCain continued with his respect for candidate Obama. McCain's comments and genuine support of then candidate Obama was profound and shocking to many Republicans. Our country was becoming more polarized. Many Republicans seemed hell-bent on a notion they could somehow demoralize candidate Obama and link him to factions of Muslims like ISIS. Black and white American Republicans made very bold and relentless attempts to somehow make the legitimate Black American candidate inferior to the other white candidates in the race. They were sometimes overly aggressive in their mission to falsely label Obama as an African citizen and not a citizen of the United States. Donald Trump led the way, requesting that Obama present his birth certificate. The faction of US citizens who bought into these falsehoods became infamously known as "birthers." But McCain, a Republican, stood up. While others disparaged Obama and his wife, Michelle, McCain had recognized Obama as his equal. As Republicans made attempts to further link Obama to Muslims by making it known that his middle name was Hussein, Mr. McCain put on a show of grace. As Donald Trump made a conscious choice to lead the way in perpetuating questions about Obama's citizenship, McCain had made a choice to legitimize Obama as a viable candidate for the presidency of the United States, further proving the good in most US citizens.

While delivering his eulogy at McCain's funeral services in late 2018, Obama suggested he was grateful for McCain's gesture of treating him with respect on the campaign trail. Obama stated, "But I wasn't surprised."

John McCain was a good man. That's just who McCain was, and everyone within and without his realm knew it. He was hard but fair. McCain was respectful, respected, and loved by millions around the world. He protected us and simply loved his country. He represented the United States well. McCain was one our absolute best examples of an American hero, and he does not deserve any level of disrespect—especially from the US presidency. May Mr. John McCain rest in peace.

In November 2008, approximately 69,400,000 citizens of all races voted to elect Barack Obama as the first Black American president of the United States of America. On Inauguration Day—just as was the case when other US presidents were sworn in—several people took the day off from work to witness the ceremony. I have a profound memory of my close friend Rodney Norman (a Black American), my neighbor and close friend March Davenport (a white American), and I watching as Obama was sworn in. At one point, the three of us stood with our arms locked around each other's shoulders in a hug with at least one or two tears rolling down each of our faces. The three of us expressed concern when President Obama and First Lady Michelle Obama decided to exit the "Beast," the new presidential limousine that had been custom designed with thicker doors, bulletproof glass windows, and other classified features. They took a brief walk, greeting a random sample of the large crowds that had gathered to support the president. It was one of the most powerful revelations I had ever experienced in my entire life—a Black American president of the United States. As Michelle Obama had once confessed on the campaign trail (causing a political nightmare in the process), I, too, the boy born and raised at the center of racism in tumultuous Birmingham, Alabama, was proud of my country for the "first time." Nevertheless, my pride and my hope would (in the end) be turned upside down.

New, Enhanced Divides

Through no fault of his own, Obama's era of presidency, which had been previously pegged as an extraordinary opportunity for change in the United States, seemed to serve as the basis for broader polarization. Of course, these new and enhanced divides in our country were not in any way connected to the way in which Obama comported himself in the role of president. As I stated previously, more of the country's citizenry wasn't ready for a Black American president than the rest of us anticipated. In fact, there is evidence some of the race-relation changes that took place prior to, during, and after the Obama presidency were driven by that fact. After President Obama was elected in 2008, the number of militia groups increased dramatically. In 2008, while George W. Bush was still president, the number of active militia groups in the United States was 149. After 2009, when President Barack Obama took office, the number of militia groups jumped to 512, a 340 percent increase. In 2013, while Barack Obama was in his second term, the number of active militia groups peaked at 1,360, representing a 912 percent increase since President Obama took office.

We cannot ignore the thirty-ton elephant in the room: police brutality. The shooting deaths of unarmed Black American men and the harassment and shooting of Black American men by ordinary white citizens have both increased. While some may argue this point, these occurrences appeared to have been directly linked to there being a Black president.

In early September 2009, Congressman Joe Wilson (R) from South Carolina interrupted President Obama's address to the joint session of the US congress. Because he disagreed with a point the president was making about immigration, Congressman Joe Wilson sounded as if he were literally sobbing like a child when he yelled out to the president, in the fully populated chamber and with the world watching, "You lie." After pausing for a moment to stare Wilson down, President Obama calmly responded, "Not true," and then moved on to continue with his points on immigration. Wilson's hubris and act of disrespect to President Obama was one of the most egregious transgressions to a sitting president and the US presidency ever.

At the end of the year in 2010, Mitch McConnell vowed that his number-one priority for the next two years was to ensure President

Obama was a one-term president. McConnell suggested his mission was a priority over our nation's security, the economy, jobs, global warming, international relations, education, wars, and a multitude of other important policy concerns. Then, for as long as President Obama was in office, McConnell and most Republicans in Congress went out of their way to block most of the policies sponsored or supported by Obama. They did so at the risk and consequence of shutting down the US government and embarrassing the entire country on the international stage.

The saga continues as Republicans, led by one of the most eclectic styles, refuse to allow a day pass without mentioning President Obama in a negative sense on their collective quest to undo most of Obama's policies—even when it means many of their most vulnerable constituents will feel the impact.

In late June of 2011, Mark Halperin called Obama a "d**k" on national television. Although Halperin quickly apologized, this aberrant episode represented yet another extraordinary example of seemingly systemic disrespect and contempt for the Black American president.

Against the odds, in 2012, President Obama defeated Mitt Romney and was reelected president. More than 65,900,000 US citizens of many races voted in the affirmative to secure the president's second term. As in his first run, most of these voting citizens were white—further validating the fact that mainstream Americans and most of our citizenry are open to and appreciate our country's differences and our mosaic diversity.

In November 2016, Donald Trump was elected president of the United States. Over the course of his campaign, Trump touted himself as a ruthless and atypical politician untethered to the typical norms and values of his sixteen or so Republican opponents. One by one, they fell off—defeated by the Democrat who conveniently turned Republican as Trump labelled each of them with silly, childlike nicknames. The following represents the order in which each of Donald Trump's Republican opponents dropped out of the 2016 US presidential race, thereby yielding to Trump and paving the way for his presidency.

1. Rick Perry: Sept. 11, 2015
2. Scott Walker: Sept. 21, 2015
3. Bobby Jindal: Nov. 17, 2015
4. Lindsey Graham: Dec. 21, 2015
5. George Pataki: Dec. 29, 2015
6. Mike Huckabee: Feb. 1, 2016
7. Rand Paul: Feb. 3, 2016
8. Rick Santorum: Feb. 3, 2016
9. Chris Christie: Feb. 10, 2016
10. Carly Fiorina: Feb. 10, 2016
11. Jim Gilmore: Feb. 12, 2016
12. Jeb Bush: Feb. 20, 2016
13. Ben Carson: Mar. 4, 2016
14. Marco Rubio: Mar. 15, 2016
15. Ted Cruz: May 3, 2016
16. John Kasich: May 4, 2016

After a fierce campaign against Democratic presidential candidate Hillary Clinton—a campaign laced with vulgarities and chants about how and why Mrs. Clinton should be "locked up"—Trump defeated Clinton with 304 electoral votes against Clinton's 227. President Donald Trump lost the popular vote by close to three million votes.

Since the 2016 elections, my views regarding the protest of the outcome of the 2016 election have changed. They changed simply because I believe the US intelligence and law-enforcement agencies who have explicitly confirmed that Russia was involved in and very possibly significantly impacted the outcome of the 2016 presidential election. As the investigation continues regarding whether or not there was collusion, I am eager to learn more about how it happened and all the players who were complicit in this war against US democracy and its freedoms.

I am not a fan of President Trump. President Trump's general behavior as a citizen of the United States, as a candidate, and as president of the United States has been disrespectful to the highest office. Trump's dog-whistle tweets to local law enforcement officers about how they should treat citizens who are apprehended by police sent clear messages to law enforcement that police brutality is OK. When President Trump referred to Black American men as "sons of b****es" on national television because the men knelt during the singing of the National Anthem in protest to police brutality, the president was blatantly disrespectful to Black American men, their mothers, and their God-given right to protest. Since President Trump's inauguration on January 20, 2017, he has purposefully contributed to the continued polarization of the United States. His handling of the South

Carolina riots is indicative of this crude behavior. The way he has treated diverse veterans—especially Gold Star ones—is another. The list of Trump's domestic antics continues on and on. Similarly, his international policies are frightening. I am seriously concerned and believe our country is closer to an engagement in a worldwide nuclear war than ever before. I am also concerned about whether Putin already has the United States' nuclear codes.

Trump's obsession with his predecessor, President Obama, and his opposing Democratic candidate Hillary Clinton is at best bizarre. Trump is strategically executing unstructured plans to roll back every policy sponsored or executed by Obama. He does so blindly, uninformed about risks to our country's citizens, the world citizenry, and the entire planet. It is as if Trump wants to wipe out all Obama's accomplishments, from health care to corporate regulations to climate change, so that he can (maybe) pretend Barack Obama was never president—a fact he simply cannot change. It's sad to watch. The experience makes me wonder: How deep is the hatred of Black Americans in the United States? I could write a book about it all.

As these modern day sagas continue, I'd be remiss to ignore how certain Republicans—including Republican leaders Mitch McConnell and Paul Ryan—via their unaccountability lower the bar for accommodating Trump. They have diminished respect for the decency and the ethics of the US presidency as they helplessly placate others about President Trump's antics, which are inextricably linked to his comportment as president. It is unimaginable this level of ignorance and incompetence would have been exhibited by either McConnell or Ryan during the Obama presidency. In fact, these same leaders raised the bar for the Obama presidency. This level of disgrace was put on display because President Obama is a Black American.

Nonetheless, the world watches as once-strong men who overwhelmingly and relentlessly stood against everything linked to President Obama—policies, bills, doctrines, suggestions, executive orders, his golf schedule, his wife, his children, his family—are now reduced to helpless, vulnerable, and fearful men unwilling to even challenge the president many citizens view as indecent, unfit, unqualified, and out of control. They do exactly what Trump says they should do. They refuse to spend the funds previously allocated for important initiatives like investigations into the Russian hacking probe.

The US Republican Congress is currently and will forever be complicit in certain outcomes of the Trump presidency, and they know they will be. Just like Donald Trump, they, too, should be held accountable. But rather than staying and doing the job they were elected to do—rather than stand up against the bully—they run away like children. They conveniently retire and go home to be with their families, as the fun they enjoyed denigrating the first Black American president has ended. They've gone back to an undisclosed norm of supporting the perceived "privilege" of certain elite citizens, in the process weakening themselves and their personal values. I guess that is the place we're in—a different form with an outcome congruent to before: the assurance of the inequality of Black Americans at all costs. While this persistence and will is acknowledged, equality *will* prevail, along with the values and beliefs of our Founding Fathers. A new day is dawning as Democrats take over the House of Representatives and the 2020 election revs up to full force.

So, to be clear, the citizenry of our country can rest assured that the Trump era (or should I say "error") and its turbulence are temporary. The United States will return to its normal, imperfect path and steady pace to living out the intents of its creeds. As Trump might say, "Believe me!"

As of the first week of January 2019, the US Congress has been led by the Democratic Party. Why? Because they netted a gain of more than forty seats in the 2018 election. They only needed a net gain of twenty-three. At first glance, it appears our country and our citizenry are finally getting the message and the truth about our current president, his antics, and all he is willing to do toward his personal agenda over the health of our country. So as we continue, I am more comfortable now that the constitutionally mandated checks and balances of the presidency will be adhered to.

I first met Obama at a campaign rally in downtown Dallas in 2008 when he was on the campaign trail. I encountered my dear friend Erica Rogers at the same event. Erica and I stood in a short line to take a picture with then candidate Obama. When it was our turn, Obama suggested we have Erica in the middle for the photo opportunity. So, with Obama on Erica's left side and me on Erica's right side, the photographer took the picture. We both had a very brief conversation with then presidential candidate

Obama, and that was that. Several weeks later, after we'd received our copies of the picture with Obama, Erika and I posted our pictures on Facebook. My image was the original image sent to me by the photographer. Erica, on the other hand, cropped me out of her version so that it appeared she took the picture alone with Obama. To this day, Erika and I still laugh about the whole experience.

The second time I met President Obama was at a meeting at the White House in July of 2014. Carl Camden, former CEO at Kelly Services, invited me to accompany him at a small business summit hosted by the president. Approximately sixteen Fortune company CEOs and other executives were invited to the summit. Each company's CEO was asked to bring a business owner or top executive of a small business the Fortune companies were engaged in strategic partnerships with. I just happened to be the lucky business owner working with Kelly Services in a strategic partnership engagement who had an excellent relationship with Carl Camden. We were in the meeting for just over an hour. In typical fashion, President Obama made his way around the multiple tables to greet each person and say a few words of welcome and for us to respond in kind. When the president started his journey around the rectangle of tables, he went to his left. Consequently, I happened to be the next-to-last person seated at the table whose hand he shook and spoke with before he took his seat. My friend Carl was the last guest Obama greeted. The fact is, Carl and I had the best seats in the house—the White House, no less. During my brief encounter with President Obama, we locked the palms of our hands and wrapped our thumbs together as we pulled each other close, patting each other on the right shoulder before starting our very brief greetings. I recall thanking President Obama and telling him how proud I was of him and to be in his realm. Then I commended him for his decision to start My Brother's Keeper, a nonprofit organization that currently falls under the Obama Foundation and places strict focus on the enhancement of young, underserved children's life outcomes (primarily young men of color). Soon after all the greetings ended, we all sat down, and the meeting kicked off. Primarily, Obama acted as the moderator, asking questions of the CEO and the small business owners. However, Valerie Jarrett was at the head of the table as well and played a key role in engaging the guests. For the most part, we covered the concerns of small businesses and the challenges small-business owners face (such as making payroll, net pay terms, credit lines, investments, the Small Business Administration, etc.). The meeting was very productive and yielded some key and important changes at the Small Business Administration—namely a change in the pay terms to small businesses working on government contracts.

After the meeting had ended and all the guests were taking second chances to greet each other and network, I noticed Valerie Jarrett in a corner talking to a couple of the small business owners. Maria Contreras-Sweet, administrator of the United Small Business Administration, was also in the circle. I decided to approach the small group and participate in the conversation. Before long, the group started to dissipate. Then it was just Jarrett and I making small talk. I was shocked to learn that she was familiar with my debut book, *Stepped Up: The Urgency for Fatherhood*, a memoir of sorts related to how and why I engaged as the father figure to my stepson, Cody. She hadn't read the book; however, I guess as part of the vetting process, she knew of it. As we got deeper into a conversation about fatherhood, family gaps, and the consequential calamity born of fatherlessness in our society, I offered Jarrett my thoughts related to my decision to write *Stepped Up* and my bigger-picture vision related to the needs of our young children. At some point during my little speech, Jarrett interrupted me and suggested she wanted me to be involved with President Obama's My Brother's Keeper initiative. She asked if I wouldn't mind connecting with Broderick Johnson, one of President Obama's senior advisors / staff members, who at the time was heading up the My Brother's Keeper initiative at the White House. Elated by her offer, I promptly agreed. Two weeks later, I was back at the White House in a meeting with Broderick Johnson.

Despite the anticipated headwinds spun from politicians, certain citizen groups, and ordinary people who seemed to despise President Obama, history will tell a story of a president of the United States who simply happened to be Black American. A president who was delivered a failing economy sinking fast into the abyss of another Great Depression. History will remind our children of a president who saved the auto industry with bailouts that were paid back in full and with interest. US history will feature a president who brought the country roaring back with a strong stock market and significantly improved unemployment numbers, which have served as the basis for the strength of the economy today. Obama will be remembered as the president who delivered health insurance to millions of citizens who did not have any. Despite the propaganda, President Obama will be remembered as a "decent family man" and "citizen" who certain people disagreed with and who turned out to be one of the best US presidents. Not because he was the first Black American president or because he was exceptional or because he dramatically changed the country and the world; the world will remember President Obama because of his integrity, his focus on the US citizenry, his acceptance and respect for all citizens in our country (including LGBT citizens), his profound belief that our country can live up to its creeds, and, moreover, his belief in and commitment to the children of the United States.

President Obama is a forward thinker. In this regard, his legacy will turn out to be less about his eight years as president and more about how he leverages his experience and exposure as president in the process of shaping the young lives of children of all races. The president has such a profound vision for what the United States should look like and how our country's values should be executed. He gets it in terms of what it will take for the kind of change that needs to happen to happen. So, notwithstanding the amazing job President Obama has done as president of this great nation, his legacy starts now and moves forward and into the future with children of all races in tow on a journey to the 2060s.

Our country has always done a great job commemorating our history; however, when it comes to focusing on the future of our country, we have fallen way short of what is required to make the change that many of our citizens long for. Nonetheless, change is relative—relative to what our citizens want to see changed. Despite the obvious divides, disparity, and race concerns, far too many citizens seem to like the status quo. For instance—and unfortunately—not all of us want or appreciate diversity in our country, even though for hundreds of years US values have been all about diversity, acceptance, and inclusion. In fact, in the face of resistance, the United States set the world standard for inclusion. Thanks to the French citizenry, we now have the Statue of Liberty to show for it.

A couple of years ago, I returned to PepsiCo for one of its annual Martin Luther King celebrations at Frito-Lay in Plano, Texas. The late Maya Angelou was the keynote speaker. I consider her one of the most amazing women in the entire universe, and I pray she is now resting peacefully. When I was speaking with Maya Angelou at the end of the event, I asked her to autograph one of her books for me, *The Complete Collected Poems of Maya Angelou*, which Ron Parker, former executive at PepsiCo and retired CEO of the Executive Leadership Council, had given to me. I have read the poems in the book at least three times now. However, out of the many poems and thousands of words in the book, a single poem of twenty-seven words has inspired me to be more forward thinking. The poem "Reverses" questions why people too often get caught up and consumed "in our past."

Black history is what it is. History cannot be changed. However, there will never be a time more critical than now. What we do today will dictate the outcomes of tomorrow and the future. Black Americans and white Americans today must stop with the overwhelming focus on our past. It's time to move on now. It's time to make the future the priority. The entire US citizenry must put the future of our children and the future of our country first.

5

Hope

April 4, 2018, was the fiftieth anniversary of Dr. Martin Luther King's assassination. For a full week, news anchors, reporters, historians, and thought leaders asked the question, "If Martin Luther King were alive today, what would he think about the current situation in our country?" They answered the question facetiously, suggesting if Dr. King had lived, he would have sat on the sidelines for fifty years, waiting for the fiftieth anniversary of his "attempted" assassination to come around. However, that is not the man Dr. King was. The answer is simple. There would be no need for the question because Martin Luther King would more than likely be pleased with many of the outcomes in our country because he would have dictated or had a hand in them. King's hope conflated with his will and his determination would have yielded the kinds of social and economic outcomes reflective of the country our forefathers intended. King might have become the first Black American president of the United States. If so, there would be far less discrimination. Intentional disparity would be all but eliminated. Our country and our citizenry would be less polarized. Racism might be a norm of the past. Black Americans would be more accountable, more successful, and in more political positions of power. Our children would be focused on garnering values conducive to winning and being successful in the US. That's how powerful King's hope was.

However, King's life was ultimately taken that day. Therefore, while we are closer, we are still divided. We are free, but there's inequality. The country is more prosperous, but there is extraordinary disparity. We have liberties; however, Black Americans have been the victims of mass incarceration and are being killed by police without penalties at disparate rates more than any other demographic. Since Dr. King's assassination, there has been an enlightening reality of capitulation in the Black American community and in the country in general. The determination, leadership, strength, will, and unrelenting accountability once so prominent and focused on specific missions in the '50s and '60s have all but dissolved.

From slavery to Jim Crow laws to freedom to equal civil rights and voting rights to discrimination and polarization, it seems these calamities are unshakable. I've been compelled to (as best I can) tell the truth about where our country has come from, where our country is, and how we got here. Moreover, it is my intent to paint a picture of where our country could be in the future. So, now I'd like to offer a perspective related to the opportunity we have before us to move forward on this US social continuum to a very different and better place for all of us.

I am mindful of the ease with which certain members of the US citizenry get consumed with the darkest aspects of the past. I am not convinced there is a broad-reaching determination of our citizenry's contentment to the status quo. I used to feel that way—often angry about Black American history. I've come to realize that, more than likely, the source of my feelings derived from the memories and knowledge of my particular experiences and our country's past. But not as much now. I understand the importance of moving on with strict focus on children and the future of our country.

Focusing on a Solution

Slavery has left open wounds upon the surface of our country's social flesh. These scars have been slowly fading; however, the indiscretions of our history still cut deep. But these mistakes must somehow be contained and addressed. Now seems to be a better time than any to focus on a solution. I know our people, the citizens of the United States, have the power to start a more aggressive change strategy—one designed to bring our children forward with the kinds of values that ensure they will appropriately and with purpose lead the way. For that very reason, I'm writing this book.

Mindful of the fact that moving on may mean moving on one citizen at a time, I'd rather witness some steps forward to a new and better country than none. Therefore, I am hopeful (and confident) that more people than not are willing to move on from the pain and sorrow of a shameful history fraught with residual practices unfit for modern day society. But for me, moving on with a scattered mind-set that tugs back and forth between the evils of a dark past and my hope for an exceptionally brighter future for the children of the United States has not, cannot, and will not suffice.

The evil in the equation must be expunged. Neither my hope, my focus, nor my accountability can be divided between good and evil on this quest. Thus, I am prepared to forgive for the sake of moving on to certain necessary outcomes by the end of the 2060s. I am incapable of forgetting; however, I'm prepared to forgive because the plan for our country's future is too important and will require keen and undivided attention. Yes, America, it's our time to move on, and forgiveness may be the key to escaping the persisting fray of a dark history.

Today, I say . . .

To the captors who brought Black Americans' ancestors—against their will—from their homelands in Africa to the shores of America . . .

To the slave owners who stole free labor from Black Americans' ancestors . . .

To the slave owners who worked Black Americans' ancestors to death . . .

To the slave owners who beat Black Americans' ancestors to death . . .

To the slave owners who intentionally broke up Black Americans' ancestors' family lineages . . .

To the slave owners who raped African slave women . . .

To the slave owners who prevented Black Americans' ancestors from reading and learning . . .

To the white people who lynched Black American men and women in the United States . . .

To the enforcers of Jim Crow laws imposed upon and against my parents and other people like me . . .

To the assassins who killed Black Americans, white Americans, and other citizens of all races who fought for the civil rights of Black Americans . . .

To the white men who randomly killed Black American men, women, and four little Black American girls in a church in my hometown of Birmingham, Alabama . . .

To the police officers who kill unresisting, unarmed Black American men, women, and boys . . .

To the 98 percent of perceived good police officers unwilling to hold the estimated 2 percent of bad police officers accountable . . .

To the US Congress and the US Department of Justice unwilling to amend laws to better protect Black Americans . . .

To President Donald Trump, for all you do counter to the enhancement of race relations and the creeds of the United States . . .

To any man, woman, or child who has done anything to harm, kill, or mitigate the equality of Black American people for no reason other than the fact we are Black . . .

I forgive you. I forgive you all, and I ask God to have mercy on your souls.

My choice to forgive has been driven by the trembling voice of Felicia Sanders as she said to Dylann Roof at his arraignment "I forgive you." Sanders made a very conscious decision to forgive Roof for fatally shooting her son, Tywanza Sanders, at a church in South Carolina. Other family members of victims who died that infamous day offered their forgiveness to Roof as well. Many of them asked God to "have mercy on [his] soul." This was their response after Roof (briefly) prayed with them in the church before preying on them minutes later—murdering nine Black Americans in cold blood on that infamous night.

This profound gesture of forgiveness represented such a powerful display of courage and strength. The experience taught me a lesson about life, the strength of forgiveness, and the power of hope.

For a lot of reasons linked to my past experiences, I've questioned the value of hope and hoping. I've questioned civil rights leaders who consistently tout "hope" as part of a solution to the plight experienced by certain factions of citizens. Jesse Jackson coined the phrase "keep hope alive." Al Sharpton, for years, has credited hope as part of the solution to the calamity that continues to plague Black American communities.

President Barack Obama wrote a book about hope—*The Audacity of Hope,* which features optimistic, key principles going forward related to elections, politics, and US general citizenship. I, on the other hand, believed most of the people who were inspired to be hopeful weren't necessarily getting the message about their own accountability related to the predicaments in which they found themselves. In terms of importance, whenever I weighed hope against accountability, I consistently weighed accountability more heavily.

I literally forced myself to believe being accountable was more important than simply being hopeful. I considered hope a wishful thought and accountability an action that could be taken for the sake of ultimately making a difference and thereby changing a life trajectory or a circumstance in a person's life. I realize now hope is so much more than just a "wishful thought." *Merriam-Webster's Collegiate Dictionary* defines "hope" as "to cherish a desire with anticipation." From my perspective, hope is a belief in possibilities. Hope represents and supports the strength and foundation of a person's will. Hope, in many ways, drives accountability.

On the other hand, at some point along my journey in the United States, I realized how debilitating hopelessness is. Hopelessness is the opposite of hope. It robs people of their will to be accountable. It makes it challenging for anyone to be accountable because accountability is derived from beliefs in certain possibilities. Anyone who is hopeless about a desired outcome might find it hard and impossible to be accountable when they lack beliefs in certain possibilities. A person must at minimum believe that what they want to achieve is possible before they are willing to act toward making that thing or event happen. When hope is understood and leveraged appropriately, it can be an omnipotent force.

For instance, as citizens of the United States, we must believe that it is possible that our current racial issues will change. But what are we willing to do to contribute to moving the change forward? Hope does not count in the past. Hope is a forward-thinking interpersonal value that is eventually tethered to some form of accountability. While it is possible to be hopeful without being accountable, hope absent from accountability—by default— may be a waste of time or otherwise dependent upon the accountability of others to make the possibility a reality.

The best way to perceive hope is to witness or experience hopeful situations and the genuine gestures of ordinary people who inspire the belief that possibilities for the future of our country are real. All my life I have witnessed varying degrees of hopeful signs, many times unaware of the actual hope embedded in the signs. Nonetheless, my views of hope and the value of hope changed drastically (180 degrees) almost overnight. I tell you—you may be surprised by how hopeful signs are revealed. Sometimes it's the simplest little thing or gesture.

You may recall, after all 69,498,516 votes had been counted and verified, a little boy (Jacob) still needed unquestionable proof that the man who looked like him, with his dark skin and coarse hair, was actually the president of the United States of America. So, while visiting with President Obama at the White House in the Oval Office, Jacob said to the president in a soft voice, "I want to know if your hair is just like mine."

President Obama responded—without equivocating—by leaning over and urging Jacob, "Touch it, dude!"

And that's exactly what Jacob did. He reached out and touched President Obama's hair. Then the president asked, "So, what do you think?"

Jacob responded, "Yes, it does feel the same."

And there you have it. With a simple touch of the president's hair, little Jacob singlehandedly proved the first Black American president of the United States was real. The gesture sent a message around the world that *any* child in our country—regardless of race—can grow up and become president of this great nation.

In the summer of 2017, I was leaving a Sam's Club in Plano, Texas. I had six bags of Kingsford charcoal (they were on sale as two-packs), baby-back ribs, lighter fluid, and some other fat foods all uncovered and exposed in my shopping cart. As I traversed the parking lot, heading to my car, an elderly white man in a big, white pickup truck pulled up and stopped to allow me to cross in front of him. Appreciative of the gesture, I lifted my left palm to wave. When I reached the other side of the pavement, the man pulled up closer. I thought he would just continue on his way—he didn't. He rolled his window down—at which time I noticed his wife sitting in the passenger seat with a smile on her face.

The white man in his deep, heavy, and raspy Southern twang, drawled out to me, "Hey! We should be going home with you."

I quickly turned my head in his direction again and smiled. I then responded, "Come on . . . let's go. There will be plenty of food." The man laughed with one of those laughs you could tell originated from the bottom of his stomach.

I asked, "Do you like boxing?"

The man replied, "Yeah, but we're just kidding." He continued, "We gonna fire our smoker up—later today." At this point, the older white man was holding up traffic. In his farewell, he said, "Well, enjoy your ribs and this beautiful Saturday, sir."

I responded with my own leading chuckle, "Thank you so much, sir—you as well."

These are the stories so important to me—white Americans initiating simple interactions with Black Americans as equals and without all the status beliefs about who's better or better off. It's important because of the indication of change. The elderly white man from the South seemingly disconnected from the old beliefs, norms, and values of his time—a man just expending his energy, enjoying his life with his wife while appreciating what the United States was founded to be. To him, superiority, racism, discrimination, and inequality are not aligned with his values and beliefs. Furthermore, they may not have ever been aligned with his values and beliefs. That day, it didn't matter to him if I was his equal; he made me feel that he believed I was. The old white man made me feel that if he'd had the time, he would have had dinner with me at my house, and that simple gesture from a stranger who happens to be different from me makes me hopeful.

Because of the extraordinary instances of hope I've witnessed in my life, my confidence about the future of the United States is high. I witnessed a young Black American boy (twelve years old) give a speech at the annual PepsiCo Martin Luther King celebration. His name was Nate. Nate stood before the audience of PepsiCo executives, employees, and local guests as he shared his story about his life growing up forced to live in shelters. He mentioned his father, who, at the time, was not necessarily in his life. Then he talked about his experience of being rescued from a shelter by his aunt and grandmother.

As some of my former colleagues at PepsiCo visibly wept, young Nate exploded with confidence. His voice turned robust with definitive assurance as he spoke clearly. "Some people think—because of my circumstances—I won't make it," he told the audience of PepsiCo employees and guests, "but I will make it, and I will be the owner of a billion-dollar business."

Nate is a bright and shining beacon of hope for children around the world. I'm confident more people will get to meet him and hear his story. Nate's energy, courage, and his determination are infectious and representative of such a powerful hope indicator. Yeah, it's uncanny and maybe a little weird how sometimes the absolute smallest of things make me hopeful about the future of the United States and especially our children—children like Nate.

Hope Fuel

On a Saturday afternoon, when I reached a 24 Hour Fitness gym in Frisco, Texas, several people were in the parking lot—some leaving the gym and headed to their cars and others making their way to the gym entrance. As those of us headed toward the gym approached the double doors, a white father and his son were walking at my same pace but coming from the opposite side of the parking lot. The three of us reached the entrance almost at the same time; however, I reached the doors first. I stepped ahead of the father/son pair, opened one of the double doors, and stepped further away so that the family could enter ahead of me. When the two passed through the door I had opened for them, the father made eye contact with me and said, "Thank you."

I responded, "You're welcome."

In that moment, the young boy had made it inside to the second set of double doors. When his father and I walked in, the young boy returned the favor. As I walked through the door the young boy had opened for us, I said to him, "Thank you, young man."

The young boy looked up at me, made eye contact, and responded, "You're welcome, sir."

I smiled as I continued to walk into the 24 Hour Fitness. As I signed in, on my left periphery I saw the father rub his son's head—disrupting his perfectly groomed hair in the process. That day, I witnessed a young boy and a father free of racism and beliefs that they were better than others. I experienced the glowing pride on a father's face as he realized his teachings had been fully embraced by his son. These are the simple experiences that invite hope into my heart—hope that despite the deviations, our country continues on a slow path to living up to its creeds.

I've been encouraged and hopeful because of my simple encounter with a white blond mother and her blond son as they came through the doors at Walmart in Plano, Texas, as I was leaving. The mother and son seemed to be hosting the boy's friends: an Asian boy, another boy who appeared to be Hispanic, and a Black American boy with coarse hair in the style of an afro. At one point, the little Black American boy managed to get distracted by the candy bar wrapper strategically placed for marketing purposes perfectly at his viewing level. The Black American boy was momentarily separated from the pack, but not for long, as the white blond mother called after the young Black American boy by name before she made her way to him. When the mother reached the Black American boy, she gently put her hand on the back of his immense, coarse afro and quietly asked him to keep up with the rest of the boys. Within minutes, the boys had been reunited and continued with their child's play back and forth as they traversed the aisles of the Walmart store.

The innocence on the boys' faces combined with their joyful demeanors told an amazing story about how the four were less concerned about color and differences that day. In that moment, they were simply excited about having playmates and escaping their chores or the boredom of being home with just their parents. This is the kind of hope that might have gone undetected. However, from my perspective, I need this level of hope fuel— the kind that suggests a broader US community will forever conform to this level of unity and the perpetuation of hate will forever be abandoned.

Plano, Texas, is situated just northeast of Dallas in Collin County. In the late nineties, my fiancé, stepson, and I moved into Meadow Ridge, a community that was still in the process of being developed. Of the planned sixty-four homes to be built, only about ten had been finished. All the moderately sized brick homes that had been erected were beautiful and—most importantly—in our price range. After moving to Plano from White Plains, New York, this was the very first shocker—property value. There were several empty lots; however, most of the infrastructure for power, water, and sewage had been completed. If you drove west, south, or north less than two miles, you would surely come across farmland populated with horses, cattle, and in at least one case, donkeys. Even though there wasn't much highway access to Plano, Frito-Lay, EDS, JC Penny, and Country-Wide all had major headquarters on the northwest and southwest quadrants of Legacy and what is now North Dallas Tollway. Just across the tollway on the northeast and southeast quadrants of Legacy and the North Dallas Tollway was even more farmland.

Today's Plano is quite different. The farmland is now occupied with structures—tall buildings, homes, new roads, tollways, restaurants, corporate headquarters, clubs, golf courses, shops, sports facilities (some of the best in the world), fancy cars, and much more. Overall, my experience living and working in Plano has been normal, compared to other places I've lived—not to mention cities I've read about, such as Chicago, Los Angeles, and Ferguson. Plano is close enough to being diverse, with whites representing about 56.9 percent of the population, Asians 18.1 percent, Hispanics 14.7 percent, Black Americans 7.3 percent, and others 3 percent. The Plano Police Department's demographics are as follows: 82.47 percent white, 7.18 percent Black, 7.76 percent Hispanic, 1.44 percent Asian, and 1.55 percent other.

Plano chief of police Gregory W. Rushin, former deputy sherriff in Illinois and former FBI agent in the Washington, DC, area, released the following 2014 report on racial profiling in Plano (see next page).

Although there's disparity in the numbers—particularly the arrest rates—the numbers are not aligned with the national rates of disparity. I also see hope in the numbers. And for that reason, I'm inspired to further encourage more accountability of Plano leadership. So, I'm sending a constructive message to the leadership in Plano—there's room for improvement.

The unemployment rate in Plano is 3.2 percent. The school system is ranked among the best in the country. The land mass is just over 71

		African American	Asian	Caucasian	Hispanic	Middle Eastern	Native American	Total
Recorded Contacts	Number	8,964	6,132	36,524	8,585	2,299	49	62,553
	Percent of Race	14.33%	9.80%	58.39%	13.72%	3.68%	0.08%	
Citations	Number	6,069	4,412	24,769	6,595	1,928	21	43,794
	Percent of Race	67.70%	71.95%	67.82%	76.82%	83.86%	42.86%	
Warnings	Number	2,089	1,651	10,601	1,205	339	27	15,912
	Percent of Race	23.30%	26.92%	29.02%	14.04%	14.75%	55.10%	
Total Arrests	Number	806	69	1,154	785	32	1	2,847
	Percent of Race	8.99%	1.13%	3.16%	9.14%	1.39%	2.04%	
Discretionary Arrests	Number	283	50	680	360	20	0	1,393
	Percent of Race	3.16%	0.82%	1.86%	4.19%	0.87%	0.00%	
Nondiscretionary Arrests	Number	523	19	474	425	12	1	1,454
	Percent of Race	5.83%	0.31%	1.30%	4.95%	0.52%	2.04%	

square miles, compared to Manhattan's 22.28 square miles. The average income is $88,398 compared to $56,000 in the entire state of Texas. Plano is ranked one of the safest cities in the United States to live in, and there is plenty to do. There are five malls within an eight- to ten-mile radius. There are plenty of golf courses. The recreational scene is amazing, with several sports facilities—including a mega Life Time Fitness, Life Time gymnastics, soccer fields, softball fields, parks with ponds, and more restaurants per capita than most cities in the USA (including New York). To top it all off, major Fortune companies like Toyota, FedEx, State Farm, Tesla, Liberty Mutual, and more have recently built corporate offices in Plano, and people are moving here at record speed. In 2013, the citizens of Plano elected their first Black American mayor, Harry LaRosiliere. Mayor LaRosiliere is currently serving his second and last term.

Legitimate Fear

I am a grown man with a confession to make. I am afraid of the police in the United States. It's not that I'm afraid of all police. I think until the pending issues related to Blacks being killed by police disproportionately to people of other races in the United States ceases, all Black men and Black boys should, at minimum, be cautious and untrusting of police in a lot of cities in the United States. While I am profoundly hopeful that things will change in the future, today I fear most police—but not the police in Plano, Texas.

When I first moved to Plano, Texas, from New York, within a couple of months, I was welcomed by a Black American police officer who issued me a citation for running a red light at Legacy and the tollway. I thought for sure the "brotha" would give me a break. He didn't! Over a span of at least ten years after my encounter with the Black American police officer, I was stopped by four other white police officers in Plano. Not one of the white officers gave me a citation. Just as the Black police officer had, with each encounter, the White officers referred to me as "sir" before they knew my name and "Mr. Harper" after they retrieved and reviewed my driver's license. They either gave me warnings or sent me on my way.

In fact, on February 3, 2008, the white Plano police officer who more than likely should have at least given me a citation for speeding chose not to. I was headed home from my friend Tamara's house after watching the New York Giants beat the New England Patriots in Super Bowl XLII, spoiling the Patriots' perfect season. The Plano policeman stopped me on a very dark and desolate portion of Coit Road near my home. After going through his standard and professional routine, explaining why he stopped me, he asked me where I was coming from and headed to. I told him how I was headed home from watching the Super Bowl. He asked which my team was. I told him the Giants. He responded with a slight smirk on his face, "Really?" He continued, "Then this is not a good night for you, sir. I'm a Cowboys fan, and the Giants are in our division." The Giants had beaten the Cowboys in the playoffs to make it to the Super Bowl.

I solemnly responded, "Yeah . . . I know."

Then the officer did something unexpected. He slammed the palms of both his hands on the top of my door where the window was completely rolled down. In sync with the gesture of slamming his hand on my door, the white officer instructed me with respect, as he had a slight smirk of sarcasm on his face, "Mr. Harper . . . get the hell out of here." As he made the initial move to start his walk back to the patrol car, the officer said to me, "Be careful, Mr. Harper." When he got in the car, he abruptly made a U-turn and sped off. Relieved and filled with yet another good example of hope symbolism, I continued my three-block drive home.

After experiencing certain situations in other geographies all around the United States, I made a choice to feature my new hometown of Plano, Texas, in this chapter. I am suggesting Plano as one of many pick cities in the United States for people of all races. There are real job opportunities here. In fact, I would conjecture there are more corporate offices in Plano (per capita) than any other city in the United States. You can count on being respected by most citizens and the police. There is diversity of many cultures here. There is plenty to do socially. There is access to more than enough restaurants and shopping; moreover, unlike in cities like Ferguson, Missouri, the police in Plano simply "protect and serve" their citizens without bias.

The Driver's Seat of Change

The basis for my hope for the United States is not limited to the boundaries of Plano. This book is—more than anything else—about my hope that the will of the children of the United States will ultimately drive the fundamental change that needs to happen in this country, ideally by the end of the 2060s. The will of young children could not have been better displayed than it was on March 24, 2018, in response to a mass shooting at Marjory Stoneman Douglas High School, where seventeen students were shot to death. This call to action, labeled the "March for Our Lives," inspired more than five hundred thousand students and adults of different races and backgrounds and from different US geographies to show up in Washington, DC, in protest.

But these students and their supporters didn't just show up; they inspired other young people around the United States and around the world to show up in their cities and family rooms as well. At the main rally in Washington, DC, these young heroes of diverse backgrounds took to the stage one by one to let the world know of their presence. They made me proud. I applaud the leadership and organizers of the event. As Muhammad Ali once proclaimed after defeating Sonny Liston when he was just twenty-two years old, they "shook up the world." This extraordinary display of confluence has—so far—connected young men and women around the United States and around the globe in support of a solution to their primary concern related to gun violence. However, it's easy to sense their agenda will be more far-reaching than anyone knows. The fact is, these young leaders who more than likely were not included in that small number of youth who vote on a regular basis are about to change that norm—and they have made their plans very clear. In fact, many of them reminded the world they have just a couple of years left before they have the right to vote. I imagine they will be eagerly exercising that right in the upcoming elections. Although I am not fully aware of the complete agenda of these young leaders, I am hopeful because they are in the driver's seat of change, and they are not going away. I was brought close to tears watching a young Black American girl, Naomi Wadler, who was just eleven years old, stand before the crowd and the world to speak up for other young Black American girls who are murdered but rarely get the attention their stories deserve.

"These stories don't make the front page of the national newspapers," Naomi said. "These stories don't lead on the evening news. I'm here to say 'never again' for those girls, too." Yes—Naomi is just eleven years old. With her confidence on display, this young woman took the captivated audience by surprise when she told them that certain people think she's "too young to have these thoughts." She continued by suggesting they think she is "a tool of some nameless adult." After a brief pause, Naomi confidently responded to her critics by simply declaring, "It's not true." She went on to remind the world, especially the president of the United States, US senators, and US congressmen, that as she stood there with the US Capitol in sight, she was mindful of the fact she and her eleven-year-old friends have just "seven short years before [they] too will have the right to vote."

The rally was led by Emma Gonzalez (age eighteen), David Hogg (seventeen), Sam Zeif (eighteen), Julia Cordover (eighteen), Cameron Kasky (seventeen), Kyle Kashuv (sixteen), Ariana Klein, Alfonso Calderon (sixteen), Lorenzo Prado (seventeen), and Lane Murdock (fifteen). I am hopeful because nine-year-old Yolanda Renee King, granddaughter of Dr. Martin Luther King Jr., used her moment in time and her presence to remind the world, "Enough is enough." Yes. In more ways than one—enough is enough.

6

Accountability: Tough Love for the Adults in the Room

Hope absent of accountability is of no value. To achieve what one perceives is possible, you must *do something*.

In the following excerpt from one of Dr. Martin Luther King's most powerful speeches, he is resolute in terms of Black American accountability. The speech has resonated with me for a very long time. For several years now, I've quoted and paraphrased this speech from Atlanta, Georgia, to San Mateo County, California, and everywhere in between. My views with regard to the content of the entire speech align with Dr. King's. While it is unquestionable that racism, discrimination, inequality, and police brutality exist in the United States, these headwinds should never be leveraged as excuses to mitigate or avoid one's individual accountability—including the profound and inextricable accountability parents have for their children. Furthermore, there is no acceptable excuse for grown men who are fathers but sometimes fall short of meeting even the minimum requirements of their very important accountability—fatherhood. The excerpt reads:

> I come here tonight to plead with you. Believe in yourself, and believe that you're somebody. . . . Nobody else can do this for us. No document can do this for us. No Lincolnonian Emancipation Proclamation can do this for us. No Kennesonian or Johnsonian Civil Rights Bill can do this for us. If the Negro is to be free, he must move down into the inner resources of his own soul and sign

with a pen and ink of self-asserted manhood his own Emancipation Proclamation. Don't let anybody take your manhood.

Martin Luther King Jr.

Dr. King was candid about the ratification of the Emancipation Proclamation and how President Abraham Lincoln and President Andrew Johnson did their parts to end slavery and thereby secured Black Americans' freedom in the United States. Dr. King was truthful in leading and advocating for marching and protesting by freedom fighters until voting rights and civil rights for Black Americans were achieved. The milestone served the purpose of enhancing the slow and tedious mission of achieving a better measure of equality for Black Americans and all citizens of the United States of America. Those freedom fighters did their part, and many of them lost their lives in the process.

Moreover, Dr. King makes clear that Black Americans own the accountability to do their part by digging deep within themselves to do something to enhance their lives and the lives of the children within their realm.

In his speech, Dr. King set the precedent for Black American accountability—the same accountability that starts with parents and parenting. However, given the racial climate in the United States and the special brand of citizenship reserved for Black Americans, the accountability for Black American children must be painted with a broader brush of responsibility than the narrow reach of Black American parents—many of whom are single parents. Black Americans should coalesce for the sake of ensuring not a single Black American child is ever again left behind.

In his time, Dr. King was willing to stand his ground in the face of fierce resistance. He and others like him made it clear—as the old spiritual states—that nothing would turn them around. The relentless nonviolent protests would continue until his predetermined outcomes were achieved. Then they would move on to yet another nonviolent fight for justice and equality for ordinary Black Americans.

Like Dr. King and the freedom fighters, Black American people and other families who may find themselves unintentionally caught up on the wrong side of capitalism must stand up and fight with the kind of vigor once so common in the 1950s–1960s era. The strategy today will differ in that there will be less need for marches and protests, as these new fights will be in the arena of intellectual competitiveness. Yes, equality is very important. However, intellect and preparedness are also very important for winning, being successful, and achieving equality in the United States. Anyone waiting on the United States to assist with their agenda will wait at their own peril.

Sometimes it's hard to accept the truth. Bobby Uncer said, "Success is where preparation and opportunity meet." Well, thanks to those who came before us, opportunities are here in plain sight and within reach. The question is whether we're prepared. Are our children prepared? The answer is simple—some are, and far too many simply aren't. I know we're not ready because we are not considered for the high-tech and high-paying jobs that are open right now when we should be. I know we're not ready because there is disparity in entrepreneurship—people owning businesses. I know we are not ready because our graduation rates from college are not aligned with the national averages. I know we're not ready because the first four letters in the word "ready" spell "read," and too many of our children aren't reading enough. We are not ready if we allow our children to make the same mistakes many of us adults have made.

If you were wondering, this has been a tough love moment. Well, tough love has its place. I go there because I know firsthand what Black American people are capable of. I would use my story as an example, but it pales in comparison to the stories of others, many of them great Black American leaders. It's easy to spot the celebrity ones. However, some of the most successful Black Americans who work quietly behind the scenes never get notoriety, nor do they ask for or need it.

My friend and mentor, Ron Parker, recently stepped down as CEO of the Executive Leadership Council (ELC). The ELC is an organization of Black American executives who work at Fortune companies worldwide. Members must be Black American and in a role of vice president or higher in a Fortune company. Among the ELC's members are Black American CEOs in Fortune companies, including Ken Chenault, former CEO at

American Express, Kenneth C. Frazier, CEO of Merck, Joann Jenkins, CEO of AARP, and others. It is my opinion that the ELC is by far one of the most powerful organizations in the entire world. Beyond that fact, I am sure the organization has more Black American millionaire members than any other.

The ELC also grooms midlevel managers for C-suite roles in corporate America. In addition, each year the organization offers scholarships to hundreds of students and donated one million dollars to the African American Center in Washington, DC.

The Black American footprints are there in front of us. The question is how we leverage them. Moreover, are they open to be leveraged?

Free Enough

I've heard the chatter in circles, on the streets, on the radio, and on television newscasts that Black Americans question whether they are free. I suggest that Black Americans are free enough to be accountable for the enhancement of their core beings. They are free enough to make smart choices and be accountable for making themselves best in class and prepared to compete intellectually for the absolute best the United States has to offer in jobs, careers, businesses, status, and prosperity. Black Americans are no longer and will never again be property. They have a purpose in this life, and their prosperity is waiting to be seized. Absolutely no one should ever count Black Americans out. Black Americans have witnessed the worst the world has to offer, "and still we rise." As my great grandmother, Ella Truitt, would say, "mark my word" on this one.

History has told a story already, the same story of a reality we live today. Therefore, I know if we do not teach our children to read, they will inevitably fall into the grips of illiteracy. If we are not willing to guide our children in ways that teach them the importance of being educated in something, our children will be uneducated and lack the skills required for well-paying jobs. If parents and adults fall short of teaching children the importance of working very early in their lives, there is a very good chance that these same children will be unemployed. If parents and adults make conscious decisions not to sit down with the children within their realm and tell them the truth about their accountability to make smart choices, especially when they encounter police officers, they may end up caught up in the revolving door of recidivism in the US penal system or, worse, shot and killed. If our children are not taught to respect themselves and command respect based on the way they present themselves to the public, they will lose respect, and their integrity will be questioned. If parents do not instill the value of giving in their children, their children will turn out to be selfish and self-centered adolescents and adults. Finally, if we do not teach our children the importance of saving money and being financially astute—in simple terms—our children will be broke.

There is no way to cut corners in telling the truth about the accountability of people. Furthermore, in the process of telling these truths, there will be no room for dithering or being stalled by reluctance. Candor should prevail in hopes of setting someone free—free from themselves; free to be open and open minded; free to do something constructive and measurable that, in the end, will contribute to making our country a better place. You should never underestimate the power of parenting.

Black American Unity

Mindful of the fact that some Black Americans may question why I would "air our dirty laundry," I am compelled to tell the truth here. The reality is that the Black American predicament has no laundry. We're exposed, and the world can see us. They know who we are, and they know our predicaments.

I've seen our prominent leaders on national television networks revealing the Black American unemployment rate being consistently double the national average. I have personally covered in my writing and speeches that the number of Black Americans in STEM jobs is abysmal. For instance, Black Americans are represented in about 6 percent of information technology jobs. One of the most unfortunate concerns in the Black American community is the low performance of many of our children in reading and education. While there is plenty of blame to go around, the lion's share of the blame is not and should not be connected to our country's broken and discriminating cultural norms. There is a part of this issue that is inextricably attached to the accountabilities of Black

American adults to teach and guide our children—whether they are your biological children or not.

Are our children prepared for the jobs in the job markets? If not, how do we change that? There should be a stronger sense of urgency here. Where is it?

I will go out on a limb and suggest the majority of Black Americans do not believe it is possible to succeed and become wealthy in the United States. The fact is, it is very possible. However, for those who don't believe they can achieve greatness in our country, it's a sign of hopelessness. It is this level of hopelessness that holds the entire Black American community back. For as long as the majority of Black Americans struggles, so does the entire community.

I cannot imagine I will ever understand why some Black Americans prefer tearing others down versus lifting them up. It seems some use these kinds of tactics to hide their own unaccountability to do something in support of the Black American community and especially Black American children.

Certain people in the Black American community need help from other Black Americans. Because of special circumstances, certain Black Americans in need of help or support only want support from other Black Americans. Nonetheless, the truth is simple. Black Americans often fall short of supporting each other the way we should.

The stories about Black Wall Street, a thriving town outside Tulsa, Oklahoma, that was founded and run by former slaves in the early 1900s, are profoundly inspiring. Back then, Black Americans had no choice but to work together. What ever happened to that chemistry?

I suggest Black American people have been in some ways impacted by slavery. If there is even an ounce of truth in this theory, then Black Americans have a profound responsibility to support each other. We owe that to our children even if we as adults do not reap any measurable benefit from our efforts to guide our children. Then we will go to our graves knowing our children's life opportunities will far exceed our own. We will go to our graves with the solace of knowing our children will be OK.

Priority Number One: Children

The accountability for our children is the most important accountability any parent or adult will ever have. It does not matter if you are a parent or not. As an adult, you have an accountability to the children within your realm. In this regard, when you are within the presence of a child, you should at minimum conduct yourself in ways that establish good examples of behavior blended with some level of authority.

While most of my views have been focused on the Black American community, my bias should not be perceived in any way as suggesting that my concern for all children is not congruent. The innocence of all children deserves our attention because there will come a time when it will be too late to contribute to the shaping of a child's values. Early is better.

Children are so important; the rest of this book is all about them—children of all races. I firmly believe that when children are taught meaningful and positive values early in their lives, it becomes harder for them to deviate from their norms. For instance, the child who is reading fluently at age four will more than likely identify reading as a natural event. He or she will appreciate the value of learning and will more than likely read for the rest of their lives.

In any case, because I have dedicated this entire book to children and the next chapters are all about them, I will not steal my own thunder. Nonetheless, my message about adults' accountability to ensure our children are guided appropriately should be paramount and at the forefront of consideration as we cover all segments of adult accountability.

Health

My mother suffered through a painful and horrid death as a result of colon cancer. Ironically, that is one of the easiest cancers to detect and cure. Nonetheless, too many Americans wait and delay and die. My mother, Catherine Harper, neglected her own health for the sake of making sure her ten children were healthy. She literally died for us. I am still haunted by the imagery of the rapid weight loss, the surgery, the expressions of pain, and the reducing of my mother. The once strong woman who'd worked around racism, Jim Crow laws, discrimination, and inequality, reduced to such a helpless being. I tried to visit her every week. PepsiCo supported me by approving my business expenses, because at the time I was managing a national project that required me to travel 100 percent of the time. I was relieved when she passed. I could not bear to see her suffer any longer the way she had.

When I was around forty years old, I visited my doctor, Dr. Juneau, for my annual physical exam. In the process, the question came up (or was on a survey) of whether anyone in my family had any form of cancer. I disclosed the fact that my mother had died of colon cancer. Why did I do that? Dr. Juneau immediately responded with, "You need to have a colon cancer screening soon." At the end of the exam, Dr. Juneau called another doctor, Dr. Odom, to make the appointment for me. Two weeks or so later, I was on one of those rolling bed stretcher things headed to a surgical room for an invasive colonoscopy. I recall joking with the doctor and the nurses walking alongside me as they rolled me down a maze of turns.

Then I remember someone asking me a question. "Are you OK?" That's it.

The next thing I remember was waking up in a recovery room and asking the doctor, "Where the hell am I?" Then I asked, "Who the **** are you?" Anesthesia does weird things to your body.

After a few minutes, I settled down when I recognized Dr. Odom. He told me that he had found polyps in my colon. He also indicated he was able to successfully remove them during the procedure. Had I not stuck with Dr. Juneau's plan, I (without question) would have developed colon cancer.

I sometimes post my annual bloodwork results on my Facebook page. I do it to encourage others to take their health more seriously. I remember sitting in on a prostate cancer seminar which specifically focused on Black American men because Black American men are more likely to contract and die from prostate cancer than people of other races. At the end of the session, one of the men in the audience asked the doctor leading the seminar, "If you have surgery for prostate cancer, can you still have sex?"

The doctor replied, "If you don't get screened and die from prostate cancer, you definitely can't have sex!"

It doesn't matter if you are Black, white, brown, or whatever; please consider these few tips:

- Set up and keep your annual physical examination appointments.
- If your family is prone to any form of cancer, get screened.
- Exercise at least a few times per week. Keep it moving.
- Watch your diet. There is no need to overdo it. Remember, there are people in the world less fortunate.
- Have a calcium deposit scan of your arteries done. The procedure will indicate if you have calcium buildup in your arteries. Per my cardiologist, Dr. Mark Shalek, most people do not have symptoms of a heart attack until their arteries are more than 70 percent blocked.

Take good care of yourself! Period!

Voting

Just as voting had gotten underway for the November 6, 2018, elections, I posted on Facebook something that got the attention of several people—many of whom liked, commented, and shared the post. I had shared my perspective on the Africans, slaves, freedom fighters, and four little girls who were bombed and died for the rights of Black Americans to vote and achieve other levels of equality in the United States. I must say, I was shocked and, in some cases, baffled and disappointed by some of the responses on Facebook and by the people who took the time out of their schedules to call me.

I was asked several times about how they would know if their vote was counted or if it counted for anything. No! These weren't children. These were grown men and women.

I resisted responding with the initial thought that popped in my head—an idea that I should explain to these adults how counting works. I realized that kind of response would not be constructive. In fact, it would have been condescending. However, I made the point that by not voting, the individuals would definitively assure their vote would *not* be counted.

Over the course of the day, as I processed the outcomes of my Facebook post, I experienced several epiphanies. One was related to the fact that not even the deaths of millions of people who fought for the right to vote could inspire certain people to vote. Another was linked to the fact that someone had the audacity to call me and attempted to stay on the phone for several minutes with questions regarding the value of voting but never took a few minutes to stop by a polling place to vote. Finally, I know people who went out to protest (for hours) President Trump's 2016 victory yet chose not to vote in the 2016 election.

I voted for Hillary Clinton, and I will not offer an apology for my choice. However, Donald Trump won the election and became president. While there are still questions and investigations going on, with evidence mounting related to Trump's campaign colluding with the Russians, Trump won the election with votes and, for now, presumably within the guidelines of the US electoral system.

So, I see you! I see you protesting. I see you via my imagination—protestors registered to vote who chose not to. In fact, I know people who made conscious decisions not to vote in the 2016 election and protested when it was over and Trump was president-elect. I see the handwritten signs and the mass-produced ones. I see the attention. I see the masses in major cities across our country. I see the diversity. I see the anger. I see the coalescing and the connections. I see the children. However, with all due respect, your vote is more powerful than an aftermath protest. Millions of people eligible to vote stay home. Why?

Yes, protesting in the United States has its place, but might more value be added by proactively exercising your right to vote? The value of your vote can be long lasting, while the energy of a protest will fade—sometimes overnight.

Family Structure

Here we are in the 2010s. It has been disheartening to witness the United States of America so willing to disconnect children from their biological parents, including watching Attorney General Jeff Sessions, with a smirk on his face, quoting from the Bible scripture he conveniently used to justify his zero-tolerance immigration policy uniquely against Central American citizens. A recent poll indicated 27 percent of Americans support the notion of separating these families—an indication of where our country still is. Slave owners were deliberate with their will to disrupt the Black family structure. My intuition in this regard is strong. Anyone who does not believe this inhumane tactic has had a lasting effect on the Black American family structure may be conveniently confused or misguided. In fact, the process continues via mass incarceration, as Black men are incarcerated disproportionately to any other race.

The ideal nuclear family structure in the United States is represented by two married individuals with their biological child or children. While several studies indicate Black American parents in nuclear families do well parenting and raising their children—on and in some cases above par with national averages—single parenting is a major issue. It is hard and virtually impossible for a single parent to perform at par with comparable outcomes as a nuclear family. It is a reality that needs to be addressed. Black Americans, myself included (because I have yet to remarry since my divorce years ago), need to step up in this regard. In fact, I believe my life would be in a different place had I gone the extra mile to save my marriage. Nonetheless, pride got in the way and may have been the basis for my headstrong approach to divorce. In addition, over the years, I developed trust issues.

The Black American community owns this very important accountability. To start, Black American men and women should marry more and have more children. From there, we need to stay married at all costs. Family is so much more important than most of us know. When I tell people about my family and how I grew up with my mother, father, and nine siblings, they seem shocked that both my parents were around and in our lives. That is a common perception in our culture. My family wasn't perfect, but we were together. We survived the South in the '60s together. Perceptions related to people like me are often misconceptions perpetuated as part of a strategy to make Black Americans look bad. But it's not all true.

While I'm not in a place to shape the will of Black American adults, I suggest marriage as a part of the greater solution to contributing to an enhanced Black American family structure. I suggest this solution more so to benefit children by impacting how they will perceive marriage and the family structure in the future. The Black American's reality is simple—our children need to be exposed to the kinds of family values and structures that will ultimately motivate them to do the right thing related to family. Just as with other corroded social norms, children are the only people who can change the kinds of twisted norms passed down to us from generations. If Black American children grow up and get married, and their children marry, and their children's children marry, then by the time they all reach the 2060s, a curse will have been broken. Think about that. Something needs to be done about the current gaps in the family structure.

Fatherhood

The true measure of a father is ultimately determined by the level of respect he earns over a lifetime from his children. The role of a father is dignified and honorable. First, it is a blessing that God made it possible for a man to contribute in the process of making and delivering children into the world. Well, with respect, it is the woman who delivers. Second, it is an honor to be responsible for the shaping of a child's life. Third, it is a profound celebration to watch your child grow up to be a man or woman—smart, crisp, clean, with integrity, and continuing the family lineage. I know men who have missed that opportunity. They seized the opportunity to have sex and make a child but missed the opportunity to be a father. It's one of the saddest realities in the world—fatherlessness. It is, more than likely, the primary reason boys and girls are often misguided. I can't begin to imagine the pain of knowing my father existed but made a conscious choice not to support me or have anything to do with me for my whole life. It is the reality so many children right here in the United States face every day.

I spent a significant portion of my live denigrating my father for not being close enough to my siblings and me. At some point, I realized that far too many children are abandoned by their biological fathers. My father never did that to us. In fact, I have no idea how it feels to be abandoned by your biological father. Now, I commend my father for simply staying. I can recall the simple things my father did that are forever etched in my memory. Like the time he and I shot basketball in the hoop we had erected in our backyard. I remembered when my father gave me that big push—the one that got me started as I rode my bike for the first time. I remember the divorce after more than twenty-five years of marriage. My father moved around the corner, so we still got to see him almost every day. I will never forget the time when I came home from college, and my father approached me and gave me a crisp fifty-dollar bill—probably the most he had ever given any of his ten children at one time. He simply wanted to do his part. However, the next day, when I was sitting with my mother, I asked her how she was doing. She responded, "I'm OK . . . Your father was short with the child support—fifty dollars."

When I saw my father the next day, I walked up to him, stood with my bony chest pushed out and almost touching his, and told him what my mother had told me about the child support. He didn't respond. He looked me in my eyes with what appeared to be an expression of embarrassment. I told my father for the first time in my life that I was disappointed in him. I said to him, "If this is how you want to support me, I would rather not have your support."

I thought he would punch me in my chest. He didn't. He continued with his blank stare and weird silence. Then he looked to the ground momentarily, looked back up and into my eyes, turned, and walked away.

The next time I was home for a break from college, my father approached me again. He gave me a crisp one-hundred-dollar bill. I initially did not accept the gift. Then he gave me the full amount of the child support money for me to give to my mother. He made me count the money in front of him. The money was all there. This time, he wanted to be sure he didn't disappoint me or my mother. That day, I was proud of my father again.

There are three distinct levels of fathers. They all fit within a bell-curve graph, with the majority of them falling in the middle section of the curve. I have taken the three levels of father titles I perceive from Theodore Roosevelt's speech "The Man in the Arena."

Triumphant fathers do the right thing by their children all the time and for a lifetime. They teach their children and instill the right values in them. They show their children unconditional love. They protect them. They ensure they are grounded and ready to face the world. Triumphant fathers support their children in every way possible. Their children respect them and describe them with adjectives like "amazing," "loving," and "protective."

Daring fathers do as best as they can. They stay "most of the time." They are engaged in their children's lives. They love their children—sometimes unconditionally. They prepare their children for the world—however, not always with the right values and levels of focus on the child's future. They fall short of being a triumphant father. Children of daring fathers describe their fathers as "good" or "OK" or "all right." They acknowledge "he was there" or "he did his part." They also point out the things he could have done better or differently.

Timid fathers have limited to no knowledge and experience of being a father. They have sex, make babies, and have the will to intentionally abandon their children. While I acknowledge the fact that certain women use their children to get back at their spouses or boyfriends, the man who is not dealing with such an issue and chooses to abandon his child is weak and helpless. Timid fathers are shameful! Children describe timid fathers as weak. I have heard children (including adults) far too often pronounce, "I hate my father." On the other hand, the woman who mitigates the chance for a child's biological father to see his son or daughter is just as deadbeat as the timid father.

No, my father wasn't triumphant. He wasn't perfect. However, in the face of the racist South with its Jim Crow laws in full force, my father dared to stay. In the face of a diminished dignity, he drank his whiskey, but he never left the scene in search of a better life that he could enjoy on his own. He stayed. My father may have given up his seat on a public bus in Birmingham, Alabama, to a random white person to and from work, but he still came home to our three-room rented house, where his wife and his ten children lived. My father, like most fathers, was daring. Given our circumstances in Birmingham, Alabama, in the sixties, that was enough for me. That's the true measure of a father. Men should also never relinquish their manhood. However, that's what timid fathers do.

Men, we need more triumphant and daring fathers. If you are reading this and you know in your heart you've been or are comporting yourself as a "timid father," go home. Change your ways. Your child is waiting on you. Step up.

Mentoring

The current US family structure is flawed in a way that has produced thousands of children who could use the presence of a mentor in their lives. Boys are longing for a father figure, and girls are hoping that someone will step in to teach them how to grow up to be respectable women with the capacity to win in the United States.

I remember the era not long ago—a few years back—when Oprah Winfrey was making the issue of fatherless children more pronounced. I attended her seminar in Dallas, Texas, at the Convention Center. Those days are gone, and no one else is standing up. The fatherless child still has a far greater chance of failing than the child in a traditional family.

Men and women, whether you're married, single, or in between, please find it in your heart to help and support a child through a credible mentoring program. While you're not required to, my opinion is that you at minimum have a moral accountability to do so. Our country needs you—our children need you. Children, who through no fault of their own, find themselves in predicaments where they are underserved need you to guide them out. In most cases, all it takes is one hour per week or four hours per month.

Single Parents

Eighty-five percent of single parents are mothers. Only 15 percent are fathers. My ex-wife was a single parent when I met her. When we got to that place where we were getting very serious about marriage, she gently reminded me, "This will be a package deal"—a package deal that included her son, Cody. Although the marriage didn't make it, Cody is still in my life; he's my son and my absolute best friend—all these years later.

I commend most single parents for their unconditional accountability and commitment to their children. I see them playing the role of mother and father in the absence of timid fathers. I've seen single parents who work all day but make time to take their sons and daughters to soccer and basketball practice. I've seen the single mother make all her son's games and buy the expensive sneakers she couldn't afford. I also see them working diligently to coordinate schedules so that their child will spend time with their biological father. That's simply the right thing to do, because when grown-ups' relationships don't work, the impact on the child should be limited.

There is a single mother whose son's biological father sits in his easy chair on Wall Street in Manhattan fully aware of his abandonment of his child—but too caught up with his image to even send a check every now and then. I feel her pain. I feel her disappointment. I feel her strength. I have also seen the single mother who uses her child as an object to dangle in front of the biological father willing to step up but finding himself at her mercy. I see that single mother as just as unaccountable as the timid father.

Single parents do the best they can. Unfortunately, they are not exempt from executing a solid and workable parenting model—one that covers the accountabilities delineated in the next chapter. Single parents, despite their circumstances, must ensure their children are equipped to win in the United States. This accountability is so critically important that single parents must go the extra mile to get the support they need from other family members and mentoring programs to ensure their children are intellectually strong enough to compete and win in a society where the weakest of us will ultimately fail.

Discipline

Your child is not your friend. Parents own the accountability to discipline their children. The sole purpose of discipline is to teach a child right from wrong. Discipline is used to groom children and guide them so that they gain a very clear understanding of how they should comport themselves in broader society. Discipline is extremely important in terms of equipping children with the kinds of values that will ultimately dictate the choices they make. However, if parents continue to use discipline techniques passed down from slavery, they will continue perpetuating the very beatings and harsh punishments that turn children into angry men who beat their children and wives. This is another one of the cycles that must be stopped in its tracks because this level of discipline does not add any value in a child's life—it never has.

In 2008, I was visiting with a friend, Steve, at his house. We were watching a New York Giants football game on a Sunday afternoon. Steve's nine-year-old son, Michael, for most of the time while I was visiting, was in his room watching television or playing video games. When Michael finally decided to leave his room for a moment to get a drink from the refrigerator and use the restroom, his father called him over. Michael followed his father's instruction, walked to his father, and stood in front of him. Michael addressed his father with a soft tone: "Yes sir?"

Steve asked his son a simple question: "Did you take out the trash like I told you to?"

Michael responded, again with a softly spoken tone, "Not yet."

My friend clenched his fist and punched his son in his chest with the force of a grown man.

I was shocked. Michael immediately grabbed his chest and bent over, seemingly gasping for breath. Michael continued to cry after he was able to breathe again, and his father said to him, "Boy! When I tell you to do something, you better do it." Then he instructed Michael to "take the damn trash out!"

Still sobbing, Michael replied, "Yes, sir."

When Michael left us to take the trash outside, his father looked at me and said with a calm voice and a weird smirk on his face, "Sometimes you gotta get in that a** to make 'em do right."

I wasn't impressed. Steve was a friend who seemed to have some level of respect for me. He had often referred to me as his mentor. But that day, I wasn't at all pleased with the discipline I had witnessed. In fact, I was disgusted with the way in which my friend had just treated and disciplined his son.

I said to Steve, "Man—what was that all about?"

He repeated himself: "Sometimes you gotta get in that a** . . . right?"

I had a huge argument with Steve before I left. I told him how shocked I was by what he had done to his child. The last thing I recall saying was that because of what he was doing to his child, Michael would more than likely grow up to hate him. I never finished the game. I told my friend how disappointed I was. We never talked again.

My mother beat my nine siblings and me with belts and switches just hard enough to send a clear message to us about our behavior. She never came close to the discipline imposed on one of my childhood friends—the friend whose mother beat him on his naked back repeatedly and forcefully with a brown electrical extension cord. In fact, the worst punishment I received from my mother was the day when I was a teenager and she smelled beer on me. She simply told me that she was "very disappointed" in me and didn't say another word to me for almost the entire weekend. That was more painful than any physical punishment I ever experienced from my mother, my father, my sisters, or anyone.

When my son, Cody, decided to fake an asthma attack so he could get out of school early, I finally decided it was time to spank him. So, I did. I spanked him on his butt with a white plastic cutting board—the kind with the handle on it. However, I never spanked him again. I felt horrible. I still do. Slavery has dealt Black Americans some bad cards. However, it's time to reshuffle the deck and finish the game.

To any parent who may be beating your child harshly as a form of punishment, please stop. There are more effective ways to get messages across to children—ways that won't cause them to resent you and, in the end, treat their children the way you treated them. This vicious cycle of archaic beatings passed down from slavery must end today and forever.

7

What It Takes to Win in the United States

Our country has always been recognized as a land of opportunity. However, there has never been a simple guideline, footprint, or set of instructions that provide the answer to the question of how one should leverage opportunities for succeeding in this country. Consequently, this fact may be contributing to the severe disparities that exist here. The answer may exist somewhere between the opportunities that exist and the accountability of ordinary citizens.

The United States is a hopeful place—a country where opportunities are plentiful. My life experiences have taught me that what matters is the accountability of people and their will to cause things to happen in their favor.

Being in a position, at this stage in my life, to give children the answers they need to ensure their life outcomes will be enhanced is extraordinary. In fact, this journey could turn out to be one of the most amazing feats of my entire life—if only people will listen and ensure their children are listening and taking the appropriate actions. If not, parents will continue leaving the fate of their children to unmanaged chance while hoping for the best—a common complacency tactic that has rarely worked.

Conversely, those parents who fully engage in their children's development by guiding, teaching, and instilling certain values in them have yielded—for the most part—positive outcomes with their children. It should be noted that the guidance of our children does not have to be limited to the parent coaching and leading just their little ones. I suggest the term "life coach" be introduced to include other parents, guardians, family members, approved and certified mentors, and trusted adults willing to engage in children's lives for the sake of ensuring they will ultimately *win*. In this regard, it really does take the entire community to support our children.

It has taken some time; however, I am now convinced any adult currently living as a citizen in the United States—even if they have not been successful—had a real chance to be very successful. This includes me. Unfortunately, I failed at being very successful. I missed it. I missed it because I just didn't know what to do as a child and while growing up into adolescence and becoming a man. I have always been a work in progress. Unfortunately, no one sat me down and gave me all the answers—all at once or in pieces. I learned a lot on my own, often the hard way and way too late.

I will refrain from making any excuses or reducing myself to a place where it is even remotely suggested my parents failed me. That wasn't the case. My parents, Catherine and Clyde Harper, did as best they could living, working, and raising their ten children in the tumultuous South in Birmingham, Alabama, in the '50s and '60s. In those times and in that place, simply surviving was the priority.

But now we're here, and first and foremost, parents across the country must start getting the parenting accountability right. This accountability should start with a thought process on how children should be developed and equipped with the values and principles required to be successful in our country. Despite the current economic predicaments some parents might find themselves in, parents should be compelled to ensure their children grow up to live much better lives than the lives they lived—even if the parents were very successful or affluent. The United States is the most prosperous nation in the world. However, our country is in many ways unforgiving. Those citizens willing to do the things necessary to succeed in our country can and will succeed. That is why our children must be groomed with certain ethics, values, norms, and behavioral qualities proven to ensure success in the United States. Parents own the accountability to know what these values are, and they have ownership of making sure their children have these values instilled in them. By doing so and taking appropriate action, we will preserve an opportunity to open the door blocking the journey's path our children will be taking to the 2060s. The outcomes for these young soldiers will vary; however, if parents get it right, their children will enjoy the journey and experience enhanced life outcomes as soon as ten to twenty years from now (but surely by the end of the 2060s). Their lives will, in many ways, be better than the lives of their parents.

For those parents unwilling to focus appropriately, their children will have a turbulent journey, only to reach the 2060s disappointed, uneducated, and lacking wealth. In addition, there is a good chance the impact of such neglect will continue to be generational. It's the same cycle that has transcended from the birth of our country. Nonetheless, this is the chance to break the cycle. The time to break the vicious trickle-down cycle of misfortune that has somehow mitigated the chance of leveraging the values and skills known to breed winners is now. Conversely, if Americans continue living the same lives fraught with complacency while just hoping things will get better, those same citizens will keep missing opportunities to save our children from the grips of the divides that are counter to our country's intended norms.

The effects of inequality, poverty, and proper education do not weigh more heavily on any citizen group than another. The effects of these ills are congruent across all citizen groups—regardless of race. Therefore, parents of all races will only contribute to the peril of our children if they continue to ignore them and fail in guiding them appropriately. This message is not just about Black American children or white American children or Asian American children or Mexican American children. This message is about the future of American children.

In the absolute simplest terms possible, success hinges on two factors:

1. Comportment: The way in which one chooses to "exist" here—what the person is willing to do.
2. Geography: The place (including city, town, and state) where the person chooses to reside in this great nation.

I am quite sure there are legitimate arguments to this suggestion. However, it's a debate I would love to have with anyone willing to dissent.

When people are forced into circumstances that require them to be accountable to survive, panic sets in, and they instinctively respond with their absolute best effort to beat the odds and *win*. In some cases, when abrupt or unexpected calamity is introduced into our lives, losing the short battle could mean that you might experience some level of hardship, or in an extreme case, you could lose your life.

Have you ever been the nonswimmer pushed into a pool filled with water too deep for your feet to touch the bottom? Then, in the panic of the moment, you're reminded you can't swim. Immediately, your natural instincts kick in, causing you to automatically wave your arms and legs rapidly against the buoyancy of the water for the sole purpose of keeping your mouth and nose above the water with access to air so you don't drown. If you are reading this paragraph and have had an experience such as this one, then you apparently survived a potentially life-threatening situation. However, had you learned to swim as a child, you would not have experienced the same panicked survival effort in response to a friend pushing you into the pool. Instead, you might have enjoyed the experience, calmly swam to safety, or continued to play around in the pool.

When you consider the fact that approximately 71 percent of the entire earth is covered by water, one would assume it would be intuitive to learn to swim early in life. Nonetheless, a significant percentage of us don't. It is estimated 360,000 people drown in the world each year. The moral of this story is that we must always be prepared for the opportunities that exist all around us. The question is: Are you willing to sink or swim?

While existing in the United States, you must be prepared for the roller-coaster ride of success—the twists and turns on the journey to making it. Just as food and water contribute to sustaining life, living in this country requires a certain degree of feeding one's mind with the knowledge and values known to enhance one's chances of surviving and winning. Our country requires its citizens to be accountable for surviving. Just as when you neglect your body by not eating and drinking water regularly, neglecting your accountability to exist appropriately, survive, and win in this country will yield consequences and a price to pay.

The price to be paid may not be realized immediately, like when someone pushes the nonswimmer into the deep end of the pool. Your choice to be unprepared for existing in the greatest country in the entire world will yield subtle issues and inconveniences—not life-threatening ones. This level of simple calamities will be realized over the course of time.

For instance, if you're that person unwilling to educate yourself or master a skill required for the highly compensated jobs available to you today, you might be limited to work only jobs that pay minimal wages. These are the kinds of societal outcomes that will be the basis for a multitude of forms of marginal existence in our country—an existence possibly fraught with plight, hardship, and a substandard or marginal lifestyle. Unlike in the analogy I used earlier when I suggested that by waving your arms and kicking your legs rapidly you could save yourself from drowning, the calamity associated with lack of education almost never has an immediate solution. The best solution is one that should have been initiated and instilled within the adult when the adult was a child. For this reason, I firmly believe our children should be the absolute number-one priority. Starting today, we have an exceptional opportunity to guide and teach them well early in their youth so that when the opportunity for success is presented, they are ready to take it on.

Survival fuel is how people choose to develop, equip, and energize themselves with the knowledge and values required to succeed. The way in which one's intellect is developed will ultimately drive how citizens and visitors to our country are able to comport themselves. In this regard, surviving and succeeding is simple. One must take charge of his or her own existence. Citizens and others visiting our country don't just have a perceived equal opportunity to succeed here; the opportunity is real and achievable, despite who you are or the color of your skin. What matters in this regard is a simple question of—I'll say it again—what you are willing to do.

I am compelled to put our country's reality into perspective. Despite how most of us tout notions of equal opportunity to life, liberty, and the pursuit of happiness, this country has a dark side that has been passed down through the generations since its independence. Therefore, I would be remiss to ignore the fact that certain factions of our citizens often experience virtual headwinds that essentially add complexity to their lives. While there are a few citizen groups who experience the kinds of social and financial headwinds that impede progress, Black Americans are the best example.

The good news is that those groups who find themselves impacted by systemic cultural norms counter to the welcoming ones still have the option and flexibility to change their situations. The beauty of this country is that it is made up of fifty unique states, all with distinct identities, cultures, laws, diversity, climates, customs, and so on. But most important are the people, the good people in geographies across our nation. Therefore, your choice becomes a simple question of whether you can afford to change your geography, or moreover, whether you can afford to change it for the sake of winning.

Therefore, success in the United States is based on two critical forms of accountability:

1. What are you willing to do here (comportment)?
2. Where are you willing to do it (geography)?

Comportment

Comportment has to do with the will of people to do what is deemed necessary for them to achieve something. However, one must know what can be done (legally) to succeed. They also must make smart choices in the process of succeeding. Finally, one must be smart about supporting the next generation of children.

In the process of conforming to major Fortune companies' cultures, as a father to my stepson, Cody, and as an entrepreneur, I failed and achieved numerous times; sometimes I failed and succeeded in the same week. But the failures taught me to ensure I succeeded in the end. In addition, I have learned that the color of one's skin often is the basis for certain factions of people to treat people of color differently. It is not just those factions of individuals willing to treat people like me differently. Our laws have been strategically tweaked over the years to support such legal disparities and norms. The numbers prove my theories.

The good news is that the headwinds created from such staged treatment of people of color are not strong enough to completely shut people of color down. Our reality is that being best in class is the kryptonite to the ills intended to create discriminatory headwinds. How you comport yourself in many ways can outweigh any headwinds or virtual roadblocks spun from the ills perpetuated from our past. Again, the question becomes this: What are you willing to do?

In terms of comportment, success in the United States is primarily contingent on three simple focus areas and related to how much of one's will a person is willing to spend to succeed within the realm of each of these focus areas.

1. Workforce development: Each citizen of the United States will be required to earn money in order to live in the country. Therefore, each citizen should be very serious about what he or she is willing to do to be developed for the vast workforce that awaits them.
2. Integrity: Each citizen must be aware of the circumstances uniquely tethered to them and comport themselves accordingly. Make sure your integrity is always intact.
3. The next generation: Each citizen must be cognizant of the profound importance of supporting the next generation of children to ensure none or as few as possible of our children are left behind to experience the worst our country has to offer. We must be willing to give our children the answer early in their lives and in no uncertain terms. In order to facilitate this exceptional level of support of our children, it will be necessary to build and sustain wealth.

I have structured these very important focus areas in the following WIN Model, which I developed at Catherine Harper for Keepers (CH4K), a nonprofit organization founded in my mother's name. CH4K aligns with the values and goals of My Brother's Keeper, President Obama's initiative to support young underserved children. However, the difference is our focus. The focus of this book is to pave a way for the complete eradication of the generational plight that has plagued underserved children. The goal is to solve this major social issue by the end of the 2060s. If executed properly with the right level of structure and national/international support, we will *win*. The United States will *win*. The world will *win*.

Workforce Development

If you do not plan to make good money in the United States, your default plan will be to fail. The best and most common way to make money in this country is to have a job. The absolute smartest way to land the best job—the job you know you will be excited to go to work for—is to ensure you are developed for your ideal job. In simple terms, that is exactly what workforce development is: proactive preparation for jobs in the job market. Workforce development involves three pinnacle components:

- Reading early in life and on a regular basis for the rest of one's life.
- Education as a child's absolute number-one priority.
- Working and appreciating the value of working and making money very early in life.

Integrity

The way in which citizens in the United States behave and present themselves will in many ways drive how they will be viewed or treated in our country. For instance, if a young man makes a conscious choice to wear his pants hanging off his butt with his underwear displayed for everybody to see, people will look at that young man and treat him as if his pants are hanging off his butt—with little to no respect. Our children's outcomes will be dictated by the choices they make.

Integrity has two components:

- Accountability for one's choices.
- Respect for one's self and others within your realm.

The Next Generation

Imagine the power of the young teenager mentoring the eight-year-old. The teenager approaches the young child with the question of the week: "Did you read ten pages in your book today?" Our children need to be constantly groomed and led in the direction of smart choices. Therefore, it will be necessary to have "all hands on deck." Guiding the next generation has two components:

- Duty to others—especially our children.
- Saving money and being financially astute.

The following chapters will delineate the importance and purpose of each of the seven REWARDS life principles, which are categorized under each of the WIN focus areas: workforce development, integrity, and the Next Generation.

The rest of this book will outline exactly what needs to be done in support of our children to ensure they reach the end of the 2060s with measurably enhanced life outcomes. I have proposed a nationally structured effort to instill these seven life principles in the minds of our young children so that they may reach the 2060s in charge and with better life outcomes (per capita) than any other generation in the history of our country. The mission is to prove the benefit of our citizens comporting themselves in the right way and in alignment with the right values. The anticipated outcome is that our citizenry will be better for it. Further, when the children *win*, so will their descendants. The strategy is to create an unbreakable cycle of breeding absolute best-in-class people with the capability to *win* while working toward this country's intended values.

Geography

You may be surprised to know that where you live in the United States is more important than most of us know. In some cases, geography is more important than the way in which you may choose to live your life. Geography is important for a few reasons:

- Job and business opportunities
- Quality of life, people, and relationships
- Respect and the appreciation of differences

During my first interview after I graduated from college, I met with two white men in an office building in downtown Birmingham, Alabama. Over the course of the interview, the heavyset white man behind the desk would ask me a question regarding line items on my resume. The first question was regarding my internship with Equitable Life Assurance in

New York City. Each time I started to answer his questions, he would look away from me and ask the younger white man sitting next to me in the other guest chair how his family was doing, or he would ask him to tell him about his weekend. The two white men constantly ignored my responses to their questions for the entire time until I decided to end the interview. When I extended my hand to shake theirs, they ignored me and referred to me as "boy" just as I was leaving their office. After living in Alabama for most of my life, I knew in that moment it was time to relocate to a different geography. After I returned to my mother's house, I immediately called Victor Owens, one of the executives at Equitable Life, who had made the decision to hire me as an intern. Within a couple of weeks, Owens made me an offer. A short while after I received the offer, I was back in New York, working at Equitable Life as a full-time employee in the IT department as an analyst.

Again, I stayed at Columbia University. Within a few months, I had reacclimated to New York City. I didn't have the means to move there. However, I knew I'd had enough of Birmingham, Alabama. So, I forced myself into making my plan work. First, find a job. Then, find a way to survive. In the end, it did not take long for me to realize I needed help. So, I found help. I had no choice. I found help from a woman I consider my second mom. Her name is Evelyn Young. Today, Mrs. Young is in her nineties. Her daughter, Mary Young, is one of my absolute best friends. I attended college with Mary at Talladega College in Talladega, Alabama. In fact, two years prior to my graduating from Talladega College, I had met Mrs. Young during the summer of 1982 when I landed the internship at Equitable Life. The executives at Equitable Life had planned for my accommodations again in the East Campus dormitory at Columbia University. Columbia is located in the heart of Harlem in New York City at 116th and Broadway. Despite my comfortable accommodations, I never turned down an invite from the Youngs to join them for a home-cooked meal or just to hang out at their home for the weekend.

In the end, I survived New York City prior to being offered a fulltime job at PepsiCo in Westchester. I had been in New York for about two years when I was called the n-word by a white coworker, John Seneca. Today,

I'm not sure if his decision was based on the fact Black Americans were calling each other the n-word as a term of endearment. But, either way, I did not like it. We almost got into a fight. I recall my friends and coworkers Dave and Steve breaking us up. Oh, did I mention we were at a corporate event at Arrow Wood in Purchase, New York? The following Monday, John apologized. However, from my perspective, I had left the South to escape that level of disrespect, and there I was in New York, still exposed to it.

New York presented me with a lot of challenges and major opportunities. There was always a lot to do. In addition, when I realized the money I was making was mostly being consumed by rent, food, utilities, and transportation, I figured out how to make money by chartering the circle line for cruise parties around the island of Manhattan. Again, there were plenty of legal options in New York to make extra money to make ends meet. Most cities are not as versatile in terms of short-term entrepreneurial opportunities. This fact supports the importance of citizens being willing to move to other geographies more suitable for their life goals.

When I traveled back to visit with my family and friends, consistently, my friends and on occasion my brothers would update me on situations in Alabama. In many cases, they started their paragraphs the same way—"Man, these white folks . . ." The message was clear each time. They were referring to the persisting racism and the discriminatory practices still in play from when I was a child growing up there in the 1960s and after. While Birmingham has come a very long way from those days when Jim Crow laws were in full effect, there's still more work to be done.

On the surface, it seems portions of Martin Luther King's dream have come to fruition in Birmingham. Blacks and whites work together. Black and white children play together. In fact, when I recently visited, I was intrigued to witness Black American children in line with white American children waiting to tour the Birmingham Civil Rights Institute, which is right across the street from Sixteenth Street Baptist Church, the same church where four little girls were bombed and killed by Klansmen. These days, the population in the city of Birmingham is predominantly Black American. The police aren't what they used to be in Birmingham and the surrounding cities. Although the situations aren't perfect, some of the schools are integrated. A lot more has evolved from that dark period when Mr. Bob at Rosie's Store tried to choke me with the pull cords from the blinds he was installing. However, according to the random-sample survey I informally took of my friends, in terms of equal pay, promotions, and opportunities to achieve one's life goals, things have not progressed as much as I had hoped and expected.

A couple of years ago, I was visiting with a close friend of our family, Kevin Owens. Kevin worked for the mayor of Birmingham, Mayor Bell. One day, out of the blue, Kevin asked me if I would consider coming back to Birmingham to run for mayor. He told me my chances of winning would be guaranteed. I immediately asked Kevin to turn around and look behind himself. Perplexed by my request, Kevin asked, "Why?" I insisted by asking Kevin once again to turn around and look behind himself. Kevin turned 180 degrees to see the Birmingham skyline. Kevin turned back to me and asked, "What is it that you want me to see?"

"You see that skyline?" I responded.

"Yes?" he said, with a question in his voice.

I then told Kevin, "That skyline has not changed since I left Birmingham in 1979." We both got a good laugh from my sarcasm prior to going inside the restaurant to have lunch.

The Birmingham landscape, with its rolling hills and some of the most beautiful trees, is one of the most beautiful places in the United States. I must say, the fact that the shape of Birmingham has not changed much in as many years since I left is my biggest pet peeve with my hometown. I am impressed with some of the new hotels and restaurants that have been erected on the north side. In addition, the freeways are currently being restructured and widened. There is a lot of construction going on there these days. In addition, I recently learned that Amazon will be building a $325 million fulfillment facility in Bessemer, just outside Birmingham. I pray this is a sign additional change is over the horizon and more major corporations are considering heading south to Birmingham.

Nonetheless, many of the same people so eager to share their stories and complain about their particular experiences in Birmingham refuse to exercise their flexibility to change their environment. All they have to do is move—move to another state, another city like Plano, Texas, or another city more progressive than Birmingham. But they stay.

Black American citizens of Ferguson, Missouri, had known for years how the police treated them. But they stayed. Consider this excerpt from a report titled "Investigation of the Ferguson Police Department," published by the US Department of Justice's Civil Rights Division on March 4, 2015.

> Ferguson's law enforcement practices overwhelmingly impact African Americans. Data collected by the Ferguson Police Department from 2012 to 2014 shows that African Americans account for 85 percent of vehicle stops, 90 percent of citations, and 93 percent of arrests made by FPD officers, despite comprising only 67 percent of Ferguson's population. African Americans are more than twice as likely as white drivers to be searched during vehicle stops even after controlling for non-race-based variables such as the reason the vehicle stop was initiated but are found in possession of contraband 26 percent less often than white drivers, suggesting officers are impermissibly considering race as a factor when determining whether to search. African Americans are more likely to be cited and arrested following a stop regardless of why the stop was initiated and are more likely to receive multiple citations during a single incident. From 2012 to 2014, FPD issued four or more citations to African Americans on 73 occasions but issued four or more citations to non-African Americans only twice. FPD appears to bring certain offenses almost exclusively against African Americans. For example, from 2011 to 2013, African Americans accounted for 95 percent of Manner of Walking in Roadway charges, and 94 percent of all Failure to Comply charges. Notably, with respect to speeding charges brought by FPD, the evidence shows not only that African Americans are represented at disproportionately high rates overall, but also that the disparate impact of FPD's enforcement practices on African Americans is 48 percent larger when citations are issued not on the basis of radar or laser, but by some other method, such as the officer's own visual assessment.

The answer to questions related to opportunities for success in any city in our country is very simple: *move!* Move to a different geography in the United States for the sake of enhancing your chances of surviving and thriving at the least amount of financial or social burden to you.

The point here is that in order to succeed in our country, comport yourself in ways that align with the seven life principles outlined in the WIN Model, which are more clearly defined with tips in the following chapters. Be smart and accountable, ensuring you settle in cities where there are opportunities for success and which are inviting of people like you. Help others bridge their gaps.

Finally, I'm compelled to remind our children once again by sending them a clear message about *winning* in this country:

- Proactively develop yourself for the workforce.
- Be smart about and accountable for your integrity by managing your choices.
- Support the next generation of children.

8

Workforce Development

When I consider the aspects of parenting, the notion of saving a child's life and sustaining it is and should be the parent's absolute number-one priority. The second priority of the parent is and should be to start the process of developing their child for the workforce. Working and earning money is the most important thing to do in this country to survive and ultimately live a good life.

If you have visited a Walmart recently, you more than likely scanned the product you purchased, bagged the product, used a shopping cart to take the product to your vehicle, transferred it to your vehicle, and kindly walked several steps to return the shopping cart to its designated place in the parking lot. You completed a job (for free) that Walmart used to pay employees to do. It's a simple indication of how the US job market is changing.

Several studies suggest many of the jobs young children will do in the future do not exist today. While the facts are arguable, from my perspective, on the surface the data points make sense. I can say with almost absolute certainty that most of the current jobs will be performed differently and with significantly much more alignment with companies' business models. Why? In large part, due to workforce development strategies at the corporate level and at the worker level.

At the corporate level, major companies are retraining—and in some cases training for the very first time—employees who play key roles that impact either top-line sales or bottom-line profits. At the worker level, students are learning more about the ever-changing workforce and are being very strategic about the jobs they choose to develop skills for. So as jobs and the job market continue to change at a rapid pace, companies and workers are in some ways struggling to keep up.

Some of the change is happening now. With a little intuition, one can imagine that 60 percent of delivery jobs might be replaced by drone deliveries. With that knowledge, does it make sense to learn to operate drones? Blockchain technology is one of the latest trends in the information technology space. Just as when the internet was discovered by Al Gore (not), you can count on there being major opportunities with blockchain technology and anticipated advancements, such as cryptocurrency (bitcoin) and more secure messaging solutions. Health advancement will continue to demand new skills. Self-driving cars will shake up the taxi and Uber driver businesses. Storefront businesses will become close to obsolete as corporate giants like Amazon take control of leveraging technology for online retail sales. Learning to sell products and services online is fast becoming the new thing as companies like Sears file for bankruptcy and other retail stores scale back brick-and-mortar retail models. These are just a few reasons it's important you understand the job market and its ever-changing trends. It's the best way to start figuring out how to develop yourself for the workforce.

What Do You Want to Be When You Grow Up?

On the surface, the concept of workforce development may be intuitive to most people. It has to do with one developing certain skills that match the skill requirements of specific jobs in the ever-changing workforce— particularly in the United States but including other workforces around the world. Workforce development has not been broadly understood and accepted because it's a forward-thinking accountability that requires people to be proactive. Most of us don't do that well. However, today, developing oneself for specific jobs is one of the most critically important survival techniques for living and existing in the United States.

Workforce development is an intangible asset. You must make conscious decisions to enhance key skills along your life journey in direct alignment with your process of finding work and achieving the goal of making money and ultimately generating wealth. Oddly, most people don't fully appreciate the importance of leveraging workforce development to their benefit until it's way too late in their lives or careers. Nonetheless, we can no longer allow our children to suffer the consequences of this neglect.

At some point in their lives, most children in the United States will be confronted with the all-important question, "What do you want to be when you grow up?" The question is either taken out of context or not taken seriously. However, this is a very serious assessment related to the type of work a child wants to do when he or she is old enough to be responsible for making money, pursuing a career, being in a family, and enjoying life.

Adults will always own the accountability of guiding children to be very deliberate in terms of asking the question of what they want to be when they grow up and answering it early and often until the children arrive at a definitive decision point. Ideally, children should be aware of the kind of career path they'd like to take prior to attending high school. Without question, children should know what line of work they will pursue prior to attending college, because the answer to the question will become the basis for the very important responsibility of financing the child's education. Appropriate answers will trigger a response about education and attaining certain skills that match the skill sets required to perform the job or career that the child has selected.

Generally, children are not equipped to proactively figure out the requirements for certain jobs. When I've given speeches at elementary schools, high schools, and colleges around the country, I've often asked, "What do you want to be when you grow up?" Consistently, I get the response from young men, "I want to be a point guard in the NBA." They answer the question unaware that a job in the NBA is one of the hardest jobs in the entire world to land. Most children do not know there are only thirty NBA teams. Second, there are only 15 players per team in the NBA. Therefore, there are a total of 450 jobs as players. Now consider that for most of any given season, 100 percent of those jobs are filled. At the end of the season each year, approximately 70 percent of NBA player jobs are filled by players with multiyear contracts. This means that college players will be vying for approximately 135 jobs (or so) available in the NBA each year. The limited number of player jobs in the NBA makes it extremely difficult to land a job there.

To even be considered for a job as an NBA player requires a major commitment with little room for deviating. Your chances will be enhanced if you attend college. Your chances will be more enhanced if you are skilled and lucky enough to land on an NCAA basketball team that is ranked or that has won multiple championships. Your chances are further enhanced if you are good enough to be ranked as a star player on a college team. Finally, your best bet will be realized if your team makes it through the NCAA basketball brackets to the final four, the elite eight, or, at minimum, the sweet sixteen brackets, and you are one of the starting five players on your team. After all that, you will have to make a choice as to whether you want to enter the NBA draft. Then, an NBA general manager and the team staff will have to decide if you are worthy of being made an offer to play in the NBA.

If neither you nor your parents are willing to understand and have full appreciation for this level of workforce development, chances are that landing a job in the NBA will turn out to be a far-fetched hope or just a wishful thought potentially linked to a gross waste of time and money. Given this reality, you should absolutely have a second workforce-development option. For instance, information technology might be a smart alternative. There is currently a minimum of 1.2 to 2 million jobs open in the information technology industry today. Most of these jobs are open because there are not enough people in the workforce with the developed skills required to work in these critical jobs. These trends will continue for the foreseeable future.

It is still possible a young athlete can make it to the NBA as a player. Lonzo Ball (six foot six and 190 pounds) from Chino Hills, California, was just a freshman at UCLA when he was drafted number two in the first round of the NBA draft in 2017. He was picked up by the Los Angeles Lakers. Lonzo Ball's father, LaVar Ball, is a former NFL player who played with the New York Jets. Ball is also founder and CEO of Big Baller Brand. When Lonzo was drafted, his father, with his antics in tow, stole the stage. At one point, he boasted about how he wasn't surprised his son was drafted so early in the NBA draft. The reason, he suggested, was that he had been preparing his son to be drafted in the NBA for his son's entire life. Newscasters, sportscasters, fans, coaches, and strangers considered the elder Ball's hubris as inept, especially since he made his pronouncement on national television. But that wasn't the end of it. Because the senior Ball was wearing one of his Big Baller caps, critics accused him of being strategic in the promotion of his Big Baller sports brand. From his perspective, Ball had made a very definitive decision to develop his son from birth for a job as an NBA player. Although the plan evolved into his son's plan as well, this example represents close to the epitome of what workforce development is all about—developing oneself for specific jobs in the US workforce. This level of development is worth featuring because it involved the successful development of a child for one of the toughest jobs in the country to attain—the job of an NBA player.

The point here is that you must fully understand the requirements (including the skills) to land a job before you make a conscious choice to pursue the job. Once you know the requirements of a job, you will be equipped with the knowledge to train yourself or to be formally trained for that job. Otherwise, you may decide the requirements to attain a particular job are out of your scope or that your chance of succeeding is minimal due to competition and limited availability of the class of job. In Lonzo's case, because he was too young, he did not get to make the initial choice about a job in the NBA. For whatever reason, his father did when Lonzo was still a child too young to even say or spell NBA. LaVar Ball's approach to workforce development represents an outlier circumstance, as it falls way outside the norm. Nonetheless, his approach is not unprecedented, and it worked.

Some of the absolute best examples of workforce development have been executed in Black American families. A good parenting example is Richard Williams, father to Serena and Venus Williams. Another is Earl Woods, Tiger Woods's father. These two fathers devoted their lives to their children's professional and social development, and not just in terms of teaching and coaching them in the skills of tennis and golf respectively. They also groomed them in terms of what it takes to be successful in the United States. Williams and Woods taught their children about the importance of maintaining high integrity and being financially astute. I have never met these two fathers, so you may wonder how I know so much about their fathering practices. The truth is profoundly evident in the products they produced. It is apparent in the way their children conduct themselves—except for a few public mishaps. But the point should not be missed. Serena and Venus Williams have been successful for one reason— their parents groomed them from the time they were old enough to talk and walk. The case is the same with Tiger Woods. Of course, at some point in their lives, Serena, Venus, and Tiger took charge of the responsibility of further developing their skills. Nonetheless, their parents established the foundational basis for their success. Today, all three of these athletes are millionaires ten times over. There is a lesson to be learned here.

The sooner children start to learn and appreciate the importance of being groomed for certain jobs, the better off they will be. However, to be groomed for a job, they must know as much as possible about the job they are planning to pursue. Unfortunately, the importance of children being developed for the workforce seems to have fallen out of most parenting models in the last several years—although I am not sure the importance of working and being developed for specific work has *ever* received the due attention it deserves.

For children, workforce development has to do with planning and preparing for jobs that they can land in the future. However, US culture is often too caught up in the now. Our citizens are constantly dealing with the immediacy of everything; most of us aren't forward thinkers or planners. Nevertheless, the need to be proactive about teaching children the value of working is paramount today. Every child will have to have some level of an edge when it comes to finding certain jobs. As such, any child who finds him or herself unprepared for this important phase of life will struggle to compete and win in the workforce.

There are three life principles connected to workforce development:

- Reading
- Education
- Working

The US workplace is not comprised only of jobs that require college degrees. Most jobs in our workforce do not require formal education and will not require it in the future. However, highly compensated jobs require formal education and sometimes specific certifications. This does not mean that if you choose a career that does not require a formal education you can't make hundreds of thousands or millions of dollars. You can! However, you must be smart about how to leverage knowledge and certain skills that may be connected to independent jobs such as electricians, painters, handymen and women, roofers, information technology programmers, information technology security, and more.

Children in our country fail miserably because they simply lack certain knowledge about the fundamental practice of working in our country. There should not be any ambiguity about this. Children will grow up to be adults, and like every other child that has grown up to be an adult, they will be required to work. So, why not proactively prepare our children and have them prepare themselves so that they will be developed for the ever-changing workforce in our country? This simple gesture will make a huge difference in any child's life. In addition, there are benefits for the parents as well. Let's not forget that major colleges are willing to pay big bucks for best-in-class students. Your child could land a full ride to a four-year college with all of their expenses paid. Picture that!

The primary purpose of this book is to engender hundreds of thousands of young children who might (based on current statistical data) be perceived as unlikely to succeed and win against the odds. Workforce development practices (reading, education, and working) along with the Integrity Model principles (accountability and respect) and the Next Generation Model principles (duty for others and saving money) are the primary means by which the targeted-demographic will achieve success in the United States. I know with definitive and absolute certainty that if young children start very early in following and instilling these seven life principles within themselves, and if they maintain the discipline to stay the course for the rest of their lives, they will live enriched lives as they grow into adolescence and adulthood. I envision hundreds of thousands of children—maybe millions—keenly focused on grasping and understanding the value of working and doing those things necessary to exist in the United States while earning a lot of money in the process. The fact is, when you know the answers to the question of what it takes to *win* and the value of doing things the right way, it's very easy to mitigate pitfalls, hardship, and calamity. The rules change (drastically) in your favor.

While parents initially own the accountability to shape their children's lives in the right way by instilling these seven life principles, it is the child who ultimately has to groom and feed himself or herself. Our children must be committed and focused with purpose. The older they get, the more ownership they will have in ensuring their own accountability is intact.

9

Workforce Development Life Principle: Reading

One hundred percent of children born in the United States are born with a very serious, debilitating disease: illiteracy—the inability to read. Parents who neglect their children by not addressing this curable disease will be complicit in their children's inevitable struggles.

Reading is the basis for learning, communicating, and writing. It is also how people become educated in terms of garnering and retaining knowledge, having a broad knowledge base, and leveraging knowledge in conversations and speeches. Adults who can't read struggle with simple tasks like following driving directions. They also struggle to respond to questions on job applications, which makes it difficult for them to apply for and find jobs. Reading is the most important discipline a person can retain in their lifetime. Conversely, people who can't read (or those who, for whatever reason, choose not to) will, by default, create undue situational barriers and inconveniences in their lives, as reading is the basis for making money and becoming financially secure.

On a different level, people who learn to read but allow their reading time to fade and eventually stop all together will also encounter certain challenges in their lives in terms of unintentionally limiting their full potential.

"The man who does not read has no advantage
over the man who cannot read."
Mark Twain

Perspective

Consider this. The skill of reading is so important that in and around 1830–1831, the people of North Carolina and other states in the South thought it necessary to enact laws making it illegal for slaves to read or for free white slave owners, men, and women to teach slaves to read. The following displays the verbiage of the North Carolina law:

AN ACT TO PREVENT ALL PERSONS FROM TEACHING SLAVES TO READ OR WRITE, THE USE OF FIGURES EXCEPTED

Whereas the teaching of slaves to read and write, has a tendency to excite dissatisfaction in their minds, and to produce insurrection and rebellion, to the manifest injury of the citizens of this State:

Therefore,

Be it enacted by the General Assembly of the State of North Carolina, and it is hereby enacted by the authority of the same, That any free person, who shall hereafter teach, or attempt to teach, any slave within the State to read or write, the use of figures excepted, or shall give or sell to such slave or slaves any books or pamphlets, shall be liable to indictment in any court of record in this State having jurisdiction thereof, and upon conviction, shall, at the discretion of the court, if a white man or woman, be fined not less than one hundred dollars, nor more than two hundred dollars, or imprisoned; and if a free person of color, shall be fined, imprisoned, or whipped, at the discretion of the court, not exceeding thirty nine lashes, nor less than twenty lashes.

II. *Be it further enacted,* That if any slave shall hereafter teach, or attempt to teach, any other slave to read or write, the use of figures excepted, he or she may be carried before any justice of the peace, and on conviction thereof, shall be sentenced to receive thirty nine lashes on his or her bare back.

III. *Be it further enacted,* That the judges of the Superior Courts and the justices of the County Courts shall give this act in charge to the grand juries of their respective counties.

That even a single slave state in the United States union would enact laws to prevent people from learning to read is in and of itself egregiously heartless. However, the irony of this is that preventing people from reading is indicative of the profound importance of the skill. Frederick Douglass once said, "Once you learn to read, you will forever be free." But large factions of whites in southern states had very different plans for Black Americans.

North Carolina and other states that enacted such laws did not impose them to prevent slaves from being social or communicating among themselves. They enacted the laws to prevent slaves from learning, being educated by building a knowledge base—knowledge on varying topics— and being intellectual by leveraging knowledge as a basis for deducting reason, planning, or strategizing. Moreover, they enacted the laws to ensure slaves would never be elevated to a level of equality or a level that might have exceeded the intellectual capacity of whites. In those times, white slave owners were relentless in assuring Black slaves would never acquire the knowledge and means to live their lives as equal citizens in this country. In fact, that is still the goal of a certain small faction of US citizens today. It is one way, if not the primary way, of supporting the basis for white supremacy.

Abe Lincoln believed that the white race should be the dominant race. It is documented that certain large factions of whites spent their lives working toward ensuring slaves and their descendants would be impacted by slavery for a thousand years or more. Denying slaves the ability to read was one of the main ways whites intended to achieve their goal. Although the original plan has failed, no one should be fooled into pretending some of these strategies have not been effective.

Black Americans stand on the shoulders of Black slaves who risked their lives and died trying to learn to read. We stand on the shoulders of a people whose will to read outweighed the consequences of learning to do so. Some slaves were whipped and endured unthinkable punishments that often brought about their demise. This reality asserts the most compelling case and justification for the accountability of children—especially Black American children—to learn to read early and often in their lives. Black American children should start reading today and read every single day for the rest of their lives. In addition, young children of all races—especially those who are less fortunate or underserved—should be reading daily.

Illiteracy is a major contributing factor to disparity in the United States. In this regard—and despite propaganda and misleading data points—Black Americans aren't the only race group plagued with illiteracy and experiencing the inequality born of it. White Americans and people of other race groups are impacted as well, and the numbers are staggering.

According to a report titled "Shocking Facts: 23 Statistics on Illiteracy in America" (Rebecca Lake, CreditDonkey, May 12, 2016, https://www.creditdonkey.com/illiteracy-in-america.html), "approximately 32 million adults in America are illiterate"—an estimated 14 percent of the population. "Between 40 and 44 million adults, or roughly 20 to 23% of adults in the U.S., are limited to reading at the basic or below basic proficiency levels." An estimated "30 million adults aren't able to comprehend tests that are appropriate for 10-year-olds." The same study suggests "women are more likely to develop solid reading skills. . . . Twenty percent of high school grads haven't developed basic reading proficiency by the time they don their cap and gown." Conversely, "kids who grow up with both parents at home score roughly 45 points higher on literacy reading assessments."

When children don't read, their chance of dropping out of school is enhanced. Children with both parents in the home fare better on reading assessments than children from single-parent homes. This is a very sad commentary. It's the kind of reality that must be brought to the forefront because it is the only way to address the issue head on—an issue that absolutely must be addressed for the exceptional rewards of reading to be realized.

Reading is not just about learning. Reading shapes the way you speak, think, and engage in conversations. Reading contributes to one's intellect via what you know and how you articulate your views in certain settings. Reading establishes the basis for individuals to couch their language in meaningful messages accompanied by a robust vocabulary. A well-read person can dictate how others view them—first impressions can make a world of difference. This is especially important for Black Americans, who experience a unique set of circumstances related to how they are viewed in the United

States. Far too often, it is assumed Black Americans are neither smart nor articulate. It's a little weird to witness the expressions of shock on the faces of certain white Americans when they encounter a smooth and articulate Black American woman or man. Our culture has been shaped that way by some of our citizens with bad intentions—some of whom aren't so smart themselves. However, the problem is more than likely compounded by the parents who question their children as to whether they are "Black enough." Nonetheless, I was especially disgusted by the parent who disciplined her child for (as she put it) "sounding white." Her child was simply speaking fluent English. I wouldn't have shared that story had I not witnessed it myself.

You may recall that while on the campaign trail and during his first months in office as president, Obama was often labeled articulate. Some of the news anchors sarcastically compared Obama to Al Sharpton and other Black Americans who had previously run for the highest office in the land. The labeling of Obama as articulate seemed to reach a tipping point with him. One day, President Obama responded to the accolades and subtly sarcastic comparisons by suggesting that when someone described him that way in comparison to other Black Americans, it seemed to imply that the people they compared him to were inarticulate. Obama was very clear in his position—he did not appreciate the accolades, nor the comparisons, nor the sarcasm. Nonetheless, that is the place we find ourselves in our country. Therefore, these are the kinds of hurdles that will have to be cleared on the journey going forward. We have no choice but to count on parents and the adults in the room to guide our children accordingly.

Parents

Second to feeding a child and doing what it takes to sustain the child's life, teaching them to read is the next most important accountability parents have to their children. Parents should start exposing their children to sounds and words even before the child is born by incorporating these parenting practices:

- Read and talk with your child while the child is still in the womb. Studies suggest a fetus starts to recognize sound after eighteen weeks, and by twenty-four weeks, the child's ears are rapidly developing. If parents get this right, their child's very first words will be, "Mommy—you talk a lot."

- Read and talk to your child immediately after the child is born.
- Work with others in and around the family to continue reading to your child for the duration of time the child is a toddler.
- Parents should formally and at minimum teach their children the alphabet and how to read at the very first moment the child starts to talk—no later than two years old.
- Children should be reading by age three.

Because knowledge is so powerful, reading provides and sustains intellectual strength. Reading has a way of ensuring independence and freedom—freedom to learn and become educated on certain topics or within a certain discipline. It affords the ability to independently master skills and makes us all much smarter.

Any parent who does not own the accountability to teach their child to read very early in life—starting at age two or three years old—will be complicit in the child's intellectual defects and potential failure at any level in the child's life. Children who cannot read proficiently or at an acceptable level before attending preschool or kindergarten will have been failed by their parents, and if the issue is not addressed, the chance of the child catching up will continue to diminish.

Yes, my views in this regard are stern, maybe because I've personally experienced the faults of my own illiteracy. At the risk of being accusatory, my educational experience in the Ensley/Birmingham school system was not a challenge for me. I wasn't given enough homework; nor was I required to read enough. I imagine I wasn't alone in what I thought was a lonely place. But I avoided the embarrassment as I struggled to get through college—literally learning to read better in my freshman year. Yes—I was forced to address my struggle with illiteracy head on and in silence. I was in my midtwenties, and while I never measured my reading skill, I was more than likely reading at a sixth- or seventh-grade level. I recall very clearly when my little secret was disclosed.

I was in my late twenties, working as a manager on a software development project at PepsiCo in Somers, New York. My group manager at the time, Joan Pertak, asked me to write a short follow-up email to one of my business partners in sales. After an hour had passed, I had gotten busy with other tasks and had missed her sense of urgency. Joan came to my cubicle and asked me if I had sent the email. I told her no and suggested I would do it next. However, she insisted that I write the email now because the customer was waiting on my response. Then she refused to leave my cubicle. Instead, Joan stood behind me and asked me to pull up my email. I did. Then she started dictating the message she wanted me to send. As I typed along, I stopped near the end when she asked me to write a question asking the customer whether my response would "suffice." I stopped writing at the end of the sentence. Joan seemed perplexed. She asked me to continue, but I couldn't. I had never read the word "suffice"; I didn't know what it meant; I didn't know how to spell it, and I was too embarrassed to attempt. Joan finished the email for me, and we never discussed the situation again.

Nonetheless, I know the consequences. So, pardon my hubris. I am simply putting into context the responsibility of parents to ensure their children are capable of reading and continuing to practice reading. There is not a single child (regardless of color or race) in the United States of America who deserves to live their life in this country illiterate or uneducated.

Children

If you are a child under the age of twenty and a citizen (of any race) of the United States who has made a conscious choice not to feed yourself with knowledge via the fundamental practice of reading, you are more than likely suffering the consequences and will continue to do so for the rest of your life. In addition, there is an imminent possibility your children and your children's children will experience the impact of your intellectual neglect.

As with other natural skills, when a child is taught to read very early in life, reading will become a normal and intuitive activity. The child who is "forced" or "made" to read very early in life will grow to enjoy reading. They will learn to appreciate the benefits and intrinsic value of reading and garnering knowledge. The one who reads as a child will read as a teenager.

The teenager will still be reading as an adolescent. The adolescent who reads will continue reading as an adult. The likelihood of one who reads becoming successful will be enhanced significantly, if for no other reason than that the right person may find the way you speak and articulate your views worthy of compensation.

While teachers, parents, and other family members involved in children's lives should own differing degrees of accountability to ensure children are reading, the initial primary accountability weighs most heavily on the parents and should shift to the child. As children continue to mature, it will become their responsibility to carry the torch into adolescence and for the rest of their life. No child should ever take the life principle of reading for granted. When you do, the outcome may be that you will have unconsciously contributed to your own lack of education and (potentially) your life's failure. This is not a joke. It's a truth, and there is data to support this truth. Children own this accountability just as much as parents owned it when the child was too young to know. Once a child is old enough to be responsible for reading, the child will reach that fork in the road where they will have to decide if they want to turn out to be the class clown or the child who eagerly raises his or her hand to answer the tough questions during class. I am banking on our children making conscious choices to side with the latter.

People, especially my close friends and I, talk sports all the time. When your brain is populated with data that allows you to roll off the stats for every NFL, NBA, NHL, NASL, boxing, and MMA teams, as well as for individual athletes, and when you have sound and meaningful opinions about certain teams and how they might benefit from specific draft picks and trades, sports executives are willing to pay for that level of knowledge. Moreover, they are willing to pay for the way you articulate your bias and objective views related to a broad range of sports.

I like Stephen A. Smith. I don't necessarily like his hubris and his loud mouth. But there is one thing for sure: Stephen knows his stuff. He's smart and there's no question about that. For that reason, I respect Stephen just as I do the sports executives willing to pay him a lot of money for his knowledge, even with with his antics. Knowledge is powerful and commands respect.

For our children to command respect, they must be smart. They must read and be well read. Les Brown, a world-renowned motivational speaker, says he reads thirty pages per day. Despite this valiant effort, Mr. Brown says he feels "horrible about the knowledge [he's] missing out on." That is the attitude that should be instilled in every child in the United States.

Because of the unique experiences of Black Americans caused by certain groups in our country who intend ensure our inequality, it has been necessary for me to single out Black Americans and some of their shortfalls—some of which I firmly believe have been systemically manufactured—related to reading, education, and other disparities. However, we must be clear about the fact that whites and citizens of all races have opportunities to improve in reading and the eradication of illiteracy. The brutal consequences of illiteracy are in no way less for white versus Black Americans or any other race. The impacts are essentially the same. Therefore, inequality that is born of illiteracy in all communities and across all races is also congruent in terms of the impact on the individuals experiencing it. That's why I'm compelled to reiterate—starting this very day—that parents, guardians, teachers, friends, mentors, teenagers, and all who are connected to children and are able and willing have an accountability to learn to read (if they need to), read more often, and teach children to read. The gift of teaching a child to read may prove to be one of the most valuable intrinsic rewards you will ever experience in your life. Furthermore, the gift of developing a child's reading skill will by far exceed the value of money, an Xbox game, an iPhone, a pair of Jordans, or a trip to Disney World. Teach a child to read early so that they will naturally read often and for a lifetime.

Tips

- Children ages five to ten should read a minimum of 4 to 8 pages per day.
- Children ages eleven to eighteen should read a minimum of one book per month or ten to twelve pages per day.
- Adults age nineteen and beyond should read a minimum of two books per month or twenty pages per day.
- In the spirit of their Black American ancestors—slaves who came before them, some of whom were killed for simply learning to read, for

reading, and speaking for English properly—the time is now for young Black Americans to rise to this occasion. There will never be a need to apologize to anyone for reading and speaking English—not even to your parents. Make your ancestors proud.

Notwithstanding the measurable progress and success made by Black Americans under abhorrent predicaments in the United States, going forward, reading will be the basis for the next phase of Black Americans' successes on a much broader scale than ever before as we forge ahead to the 2060s. However, the best way to ensure that broad, successful milestones are achieved is for adults to engage our children. The Black American community must treat the very important skill of reading as a lifeline and the single most important attribute required for Black American children (or any child) to survive and strive in our country—as they, too, were born with the inalienable right to pursue happiness.

10

Workforce Development Life Principle: Education

Education is the second of three life principles in the Workforce Development Model. Because education has to do with learning certain skills required to work on certain jobs, it is the backbone of workforce development. In fact, education is the only way people can be developed for the workforce, start-up businesses, or any jobs as an independent contractor.

Merriam-Webster's defines "educate" as follows:

1. "To train by formal instruction and supervised practice especially in a skill trade or profession."
2. "To provide with information: INFORM."

The key to being developed for the workforce is to first become educated on the different categories or disciplines associated with certain work. Once a person gains a good understanding of the different tiers of jobs in the workforce, the next natural thing to do will be to figure out the skills required to perform in a certain category of work. Next, the person will have to master the skills required for the work they have chosen. For instance, if you decide you want to be a landscaper, you will have to master the skills of grooming lawns and planting and maintaining flowerbeds. On the other hand, if you make a conscious decision that you want to become CEO of a Fortune company, be prepared to attain, at minimum, a bachelor's degree and a master's degree within a discipline such as finance, marketing, or operations.

Perspective

Education is critical to winning in this country. Education is the second-most important attribute any person should have instilled within them—second only to reading. Being educated on any subject or skill, especially if you become best in class in a demanded skill such as internet security, will enhance your positioning for some level of success in our country. Sadly, just as with reading, I am compelled to put into perspective certain truths related to those in our country who have, over the years, persisted in their quest to mitigate chances for Black Americans to be educated.

In the 1960s, factions of our citizens made attempts in the South to perpetuate historic norms ensuring the inequality of Black Americans. They went as far as to ensure Black Americans would not be educated in the same manner, at the same level, or at the same schools as whites. You may recall the segregation laws of the era. On January 14, 1963, after winning the governorship of Alabama, Governor George Wallace stood at a podium to deliver his inaugural address. I have no idea what the rest of the speech was about. However, I can still hear the infamous words, etched in my memory with Wallace's southern twang. As he described his vision for the segregation of public schools and other institutions in Alabama, he egregiously commented, "Segregation today, segregation tomorrow, and segregation forever."

Thirty years or so later, after falling short of his segregation goals, the former governor of Alabama apologized to some of the same people he had attempted to impose his power against by moderating their progress and chances of being educated. He whispered to the group from his wheelchair, "I love you."

But we've moved on from those times and those kinds of barriers to learning. Citizens in this country are free to learn whatever they choose. They have access to libraries all across the country. Thousands of colleges and universities are waiting with open arms to process your applications. There are trade schools and apprentice programs where anyone willing can master certain blue-collar skills. There are specific technology certifications that anyone can train for and become certified in, such as project management. There is no state governor willing to stand at the entrance of major colleges and universities to prevent Black Americans or any other citizen group from attending. However, in many cases, if your plan is to attend the absolute best colleges or universities, cost becomes the barrier. Nonetheless, because of broad access to affordable informal and formal education in our country, people unwilling to be educated do so by choice and will risk missing opportunities to fully pursue their own happiness. They do so at their own peril.

The unemployment rate for Black Americans has consistently been double the national unemployment rate. Although a part of the problem may be linked to systemic and isolated discrimination, the question of whether education is a contributing factor is a valid one.

Today, Black Americans represent only about 7.4 percent of employees in information technology (IT) jobs. In addition, there are millions of IT jobs open right now because our citizens do not have the skills required in these high-tech, high-paying jobs. My experience as senior manager in the IT field, as an entrepreneur, and as head of a company that provides recruiting services to fill IT jobs has taught me one simple fact. When you are best in class, color does not matter anymore. Race does not matter. In some cases, it doesn't even matter if you wear shorts and flip-flops to work while you present to a Fortune company's board of directors. What matters is your knowledge, your skill, and your role as the top IT security person responsible for protecting corporate data from hackers willing to take the information to use for their personal gain or for reasons that could have negative impacts on the victimized company.

Our children have an accountability to take charge of their will to develop themselves intellectually. Each child must beat the odds by proactively strengthening their intellectual foundation and power by honing those skills that are in high demand and highly compensated. It is a proven fact that, given the right focus, any child can establish themselves among the best in class in IT and other skills of value. Yeah—I am a little biased about this one; Black American children should be out in front and ahead of the curve in terms of making reading and education their absolute number-one and number-two priorities respectively. By doing so, finding highly compensating jobs will be easy, and the value of their knowledge will be measurably elevated. In addition, their chances of making it to the 2060s with enhanced life outcomes will be significantly improved day by day, week by week, and year by year.

Parents

My son, Cody, got in trouble in school for being the class clown. His mother (Sara) and I received the news while attending a parent/teacher conference at his school. When we returned home, we discussed the issue and agreed on my suggestion to punish Cody by making him write the sentence "My education is my number-one priority" one thousand times. We discussed the issue and the punishment with Cody over dinner that evening. Cody wasn't happy. After dinner, we told him to go to his room to get started on his project. It was a Friday night. After he had been in his room writing for over an hour, I decided to check on him to see how his progress was going. What I found was unexpected and very disappointing. Cody had written the word "My" all the way down the left side of at least twenty-five to thirty pages. Next to the word "My" he had written the word "education" all the way down the same number of pages. I think I may have caught him just in time before he started to write the word "is" next to the word "education" all the way down those same pages.

I immediately apologized to Cody and told him how sorry I was and that it was my fault for not being clear with my instructions. In the process of letting my son know he had to start all over again, I politely asked Cody to tear up the pages he had written. With his mouth wide open, the tears started to roll down his face. Again, Cody wasn't happy.

This time, I was very clear with my instructions. I told Cody he needed to write the entire sentence—"My education is my number-one priority"— before moving to the next line to write the same sentence over again. Then I explained to Cody the reason he needed to start over was because his mom and I were concerned he would not get the clear message we were trying to convey to him if we allowed him to write the sentence his way—one word at a time. Sara and I needed to be sure Cody got the message that his education was his absolute number-one priority! In the end, Cody got the message. I'm not taking credit; Cody is without question *the* smartest young adult I know. Many of my friends agree.

All parents are not created equal. Most parents are not financially established at levels that would allow them to cover the tuition at Harvard, Yale, Columbia, and many other colleges and universities. However, education is not just about being a product of an Ivy League university. Being educated is not about a requirement to attain a college degree. Being educated is simply being smart about one's capacity to attain knowledge that can be leveraged for earning a living. In this regard, parents have profound early opportunities to teach and groom their children in the process of ensuring they will be developed for a workforce that includes jobs at all levels. To be successful in this important responsibility, parents should be relentless in their determination to understand the workforce so that they are equipped with the knowledge to appropriately lead their children in their decisions regarding what they want to be when they grow up.

My mother was always on my siblings and me about our education and reading. On the other hand, as I've already said, my father was a man of few words. However, when I graduated from Talladega College in Alabama, to my surprise, my father attended my graduation. He never told me or the rest of my family he was planning to attend, and no one knows how he got there. He just showed up.

I was shocked to see my father there. When I was in line to walk onstage to receive my diploma, I noticed security talking to a tall, dark man who had penetrated the secured area around the stage. The man was somewhat animated—seemingly with determination to go on stage. Then I noticed it was my "daddy." To this day, I have no idea what my father was saying to the security guards. But, in the end, they allowed him to stand at the bottom of the steps on the opposite end of the stage from where I was. Several of my classmates received their diplomas ahead of me. Then it was my turn. When the announcer called my name, I gracefully walked across the stage to receive my diploma. I could hear the few cheers from some of my friends, my mother, my aunt Elma, and my siblings who had attended. As I reached the president of Talladega, who had my diploma in his left hand and his right hand extended out to me, I reached out, shook his hand with my right one, and received my diploma with my left. After he congratulated me, I continued to walk to the other side of the stage and down the steps, where my father was proudly and anxiously awaiting my arrival. As I reached the last few steps, I witnessed for the first time a tear fall from my father's left eye. Then I witnessed the second tear fall from the left eye, and from that point, I lost count. My father hugged me for what seemed to be an eternity. While we were still embraced, he congratulated me. Then, just before I was instructed to return to my seat, he whispered in my ear, "Son, your education—it's the one thing they will never be able to take away from you." And while I had previously heard the same message from my father before, somehow his tears forced me to take him more seriously. But was it too late? It was in that moment I realized I had missed so many opportunities to take education more seriously.

Electrician in Training

I hired a certified electrician to run a few electrical drops in my garage for a project my son, Cody, and I had initiated. The young man happened to be Hispanic. Near the end of his visit, he realized he had forgotten to buy a certain part required to complete the job. He asked if it would be OK if he returned on Saturday to complete the work. I agreed. On Saturday, when he returned in his truck with his logos prominently displayed on each door, the man was in the passenger seat. His son, who looked to be just old enough to drive, was behind the wheel.

As the father/son (and teacher/pupil) played their roles, it became obvious what was happening. The pupil, the man's son, was being groomed to be a certified electrical technician. His father was teaching him everything he needed to know about being a technician. So, while the young boy's friends were probably somewhere playing on that beautiful Saturday morning, this young boy was being educated and developed for the job he was destined to do in the US workforce. I am sure the father also told his son exactly how much money he commanded because he had become a certified expert in the field of electricity. The average hourly rate for a certified electrician is $50 to $100 per hour. He also had to tell his son about the risks associated with being an electrician. I imagine the man had taught his son all he knew about customer service because when the job was done and I had paid them for the work they had completed, they both shook my hand one by one and said, "Thank you, sir," before they got back in their truck and moved on to their next customer.

On the other hand, the parent who has successfully matriculated through an MBA program will more than likely take a very different approach to grooming their child for the workforce. They might ensure their child is being prepped for college. In addition, they will make sure their child is planning to work in at least two internship programs at major Fortune companies.

I have interviewed far too many college students applying for full-time work at PepsiCo who did not have work experience and were competing with other students who had legitimate corporate jobs on their resumes. Consider two college graduates, both with 4.0 grade point averages, bachelor's degrees in information systems, and solid school project work and generally matched in terms of skill. However, one of them has two summer internships at two different Fortune companies on his or her resume. Which one will be hired first? The one with the most real-life work experience.

If your child is planning to work in corporate America, please be sure to guide them accordingly so that they are prepared to compete with the best. The combination of education and work experience will be the basis for career growth in corporate America. In this regard, children planning for careers in this area must also plan to complete a minimum of two internships, ideally at major Fortune companies like PepsiCo, Amazon, Google, American Express, or World Wide Technology. Your choices will be endless. However, you must be aggressive and proactive about your plan.

It doesn't matter the level of job or the discipline you become interested in; having a plan to land that job is extremely important. Either way, parents are the ones who should be leading their children in the early stages of this structured approach to their child being developed for any job in the workforce. Remember the story of the father and son electricians.

Children

The value of knowing or attaining knowledge is zero. The value of knowing will remain zero until such time as the person with the knowledge leverages what they know to add some level of value, either monetary or intrinsic.

In this country, people need education and knowledge instilled in them to be successful in landing any level of work. In fact, it really doesn't matter what country you're in; education and knowledge are and will forever be the intangible enablers to earning well-paying jobs. Therefore, the application of the knowledge you retain is the only way to make that knowledge of any value. Consider the medical doctor who makes a conscious choice not to practice medicine or share his or her knowledge. That doctor will retain those expensive, invaluable skills until he or she decides to do something to monetize the knowledge.

In the process of developing yourself for the workforce, whatever career path you decide to take, it's important you establish your foundational education and knowledge base.

Education is a prerequisite to work. In the process of determining the job or line of work you want to be involved in for the sake of making a living and pursuing a career, you must first gain a very clear understanding of the work by determining the following:

- **Your value.** What value are you seeking to attain for yourself, and (potentially) your family in the short-term, midterm, and long-term?
- The **education and skills** required for you to achieve your goal of landing your ideal job—whether it's that evasive job as an NBA player, the CEO of a Fortune company, a welder, an expert landscaper, or an entrepreneur owning a company.
- **Your will** in terms of comportment and geography—your commitment to doing what it takes to achieve your goals related to living, your lifestyle, and your plan to build wealth. Are you willing to move to a different geography—including a different country?

Value

Mika Brzezinski, host of *The Morning Joe Show*, spearheaded a national and worldwide conference titled "Know Your Value." Although the primary demographic targeted was women, the notion of children knowing their value applies to every child and every teenager within the boundaries of the United States and around the world.

Children should start planning very early in life rather than doing what I did, which is leaving their lives to chance. You first must figure out, in relative terms, what you need, at minimum, to live comfortably. Teenagers should start thinking early about whether or not they will have a family. This level of planning will contribute significantly to the teenager understanding his or her value. Finally, teens must consider as they grow older whether they will play roles supporting other children of the next generations. If so, at what level will they support them?

Answers to these kinds of questions early in life will help to shape your value and your will to be educated and do what it takes to master your life plan.

Education Skills and Levels

Teenagers must gain a clear understanding, via research, what formal and/ or informal education will be required of them to land their ideal jobs. They must gain and hone knowledge related to the skill requirements for certain jobs and entrepreneurial opportunities, such as becoming a certified financial advisor, or an electrician, or an owner of a fast-food franchise. Much of this research can be attained with a simple Google search.

If your interest is in the information technology field, you may already know that high-tech companies like Google, Apple, Facebook, Amazon, Uber, Microsoft, and World Wide Technology hire highly skilled IT employees every day. Many of the companies hire employees right out of college in the high five-figure range—$65,000 to $90,000 annually and possibly more. Definitely more if you have a master's degree, such as an MBA. In addition, many job openings are available in the IT arena. Beyond the tech companies, major Fortune companies like PepsiCo (which includes Pepsi, Frito-Lay, Quaker, Gatorade, and Tropicana) compensate employees very well and in alignment with market values. Graduating students who land jobs with companies like these are successful because they proactively place focus on clearly understanding the skills required. Then they determine whether the job and the related compensation is in alignment with their values. When students get the idea of educating themselves for key jobs in the workplace that compensate well, they often get to choose what company they land at and more than likely provide input in terms of their value.

What Are You Willing to Do?

One might think this question is simple. It's not, because the answer implies a very serious commitment to taking actions toward laying the foundation for the rest of your life. So, what are you willing to do to land your ideal job or start a business? If your ideal career is a job in the NBA as a player, if you didn't start playing basketball at age three, it may be too late. Do you think you can become a top high school basketball player in a very competitive basketball market and make the national tournaments (like the McDonald's Championship)? Do you think you can successfully beat out players in the national college arena, traverse the brackets, and make it to the final four? Moreover, are you willing to commit to these stringent requirements while maintaining a minimum GPA of 3.5 in the process of completing your bachelor's degree? If you are not willing or if you do not consider yourself capable of achieving these kinds of milestones required to be considered to play in the NBA, *do not* waste your time. Consider a different field, and keep in mind: your education is your number-one priority.

Tips

- **Continue reading**. Read on a regular basis. I cannot stress the importance of reading enough. In many ways, it doesn't matter what you read or the genre. However, I suggest you read with some level of purpose. Read the Bible, fiction, nonfiction, self-help, romance, comedy, politics, history, news (the *Wall Street Journal, USA Today,* the *Washington Post,* and the *New York Times*), biographies, tragedy, adventure, mystery, the classics, or whatever you choose. Just read, because, again, reading is the basis for learning and educating yourself. However, with purposeful reading, it is possible you can sit in a basement, learn a skill like computer programming, and become best in class at whichever programming language you decide to learn. Just be mindful of the most current programming technologies, as it might be a waste of your time to learn a language like Java. By doing so, as a teenager, you could become the next Bill Gates or Mark Zuckerberg.

- **Attain a minimum of a bachelor's degree.** At least consider it. While attaining a bachelor's degree is not required for success in our country, if for whatever reason your ideal entrepreneurial strategy should fail, you'll always have one of the minimal requirements for a good-paying job to fall back on. Achieving a degree in business administration would be a smart choice because everyone needs to understand how to run and manage a business—including the financial aspects of a business. In addition, major corporations will accept a bachelor's degree in business administration as a minimal requirement.
- Owning a business is easier than you may think. Most people don't realize it, but each time you balance your checking account, you are managing a balance sheet. What you have as cash are your assets. What you owe in terms of bills are your liabilities. The difference between the assets and liabilities is equity. Therefore, assets = liabilities + equity. Understanding the concept of the balance sheet will be key to running your own business, as the balance sheet is the model that is used to measure the net worth of any business.
- Another intellectual discipline worth attaining would be a degree in information technology or business systems. Why? Because there are and will continue to be excellent career opportunities in the information technology space today and for the foreseeable future. If not a bachelor's degree, at minimum attain a specialized skill, such as information technology security. Attain certifications, including certifications in project management tools such as Agile.
- Consider formal training which focus on certifications in real estate, plumbing, roofing, electricity, etc. Some of these fields can be very lucrative as an individual contributor or contractor.
- **Learn a second language.** It is uncanny and somewhat bizarre witnessing a president of the United States publicly demanding that "certain" immigrants coming to our country must first be fluent in English. It's strange because when the same president visits other non-English speaking countries, he requires a translator to understand the

different languages, such as Spanish, French, or Chinese. But this is not a problem that starts and stops at the current presidency. It's a common flaw in the US, as we—myself included—have simply refused to learn other languages. Going into the 2060s, all children must step up and change this disastrous US norm. You must redirect this double-standard philosophy by changing the current trajectory toward a new path to a more serious eventual "exceptionalism" that aligns with stated US core values. As our young boys and girls grow up to be young men and young women, they must be equipped with everything it takes to compete in global markets and geographies. Times are changing, and the status quo is no longer sustainable nor adequate going forward. More citizens of other foreign nations speak English as a second language than not. We must be ready as well!

11

Workforce Development Life Principle: Work

As I've already stated, making reading and education the top priorities is the first step required for any child to be developed for the US workforce. Furthermore, our children need to be taught the value of money. The simple notion of teaching a child for the first time that they can earn money for doing something productive can be a very compelling experience. Working and appreciating the value of working early is also key to being prepared for jobs in the workforce. Work is the third and final life principle in the Workforce Development Model.

If you are a citizen of the United States who is not affluent or born into wealth, you will be required to work in order to survive and pursue happiness in our country. The United States, with all its glamour, prosperity, and varying levels of freedom, can be unforgiving.

The will of US citizens to act in the process of developing useful skills will be key to their success in the workforce. In this country, work is legal within a broad range, including jobs where all it takes is for the worker to press a single key on a keyboard with their index finger and, in that simple step, earn millions of dollars. On the other end of the spectrum, consider the worker whose job requires her or him to lift and move more than fifty pounds of product in a warehouse repeatedly over the course of an eight-hour day shift. Then, there are all the jobs between. The good news is that the job you land is, for the most part, solely up to you and your will to do what it takes to work in the job you perceive as the best one for you, your goals, and your family.

Social programs are necessary and serve a purpose in our society. There are diverse groups of citizens who are willing to go the extra mile to secure the benefits of government programs such as welfare and food stamps to mitigate working. In addition, I am quite sure I have given money to men or women who would rather panhandle than find a legitimate job and go to work or start a small business like mowing lawns. I give these individuals a little cash when I have it readily available because I'm not always sure whether they need food to survive. In any case, these kinds of strategies for collecting money outside the normal workforce have never been sustainable for living in our country. Work is the only legitimate and proven answer to living and existing.

Perspective

Work is what sustains the US economy. The concept of supply and demand is what fuels an economy. When customers demand certain products, companies have opportunities to supply that product to the marketplace. In a normal work model, people are usually hired and paid for meeting the demands of consumers. Contrary to certain theories touted by politicians on the right, chief executive officers (CEOs) or chief financial officers (CFOs) at major companies do not check the cash line on their balance sheets, yet they're the ones making decisions to hire people. Under normal circumstances, companies hire human resources for the purpose of creating and meeting the demands of the products and services they offer.

I grew up witnessing my mother and father work hard as hell for their ten children. Even as a child, I wanted to do something, however minimal, to take some of the burden off my mother.

I learned the value of working very early in my life. My very first job was paper delivery when I was around seven years old. When I was old enough, I started mowing the neighbor's (Mrs. Smith's) front and back yards and trimming the hedges with manual clippers for just five dollars. The job took me almost a full day to complete. When I was in my first year in high school, one day after class my biology teacher, Mr. Sampson Julius Bennett, approached me. He asked, "Boy, you want a job?"

His aggressive tone scared me. Still, perplexed by his aggression and my desperation for money, I responded immediately, "Yes, sir."

I had no idea what Mr. Bennett had in mind; however, if making some extra money was involved, I was completely open. I was also aware that at least two of my older brothers had worked for Mr. Bennett at Prince Hall Apartments in Ensley. It was rumored the Bennetts owned the thirteen-building apartment campus. After I agreed, Mr. Bennett instructed me to meet him at the apartment office immediately after school. So I did, and with my mother's consent, I was hired for my first legitimate job. For the next four years, I mowed the lawn and made sure the grounds at Prince Hall Apartments were groomed every day—including Saturdays.

My first job in college was in the financial aid office at Talladega College. I guess I was smart enough to realize that if you didn't have any money for college, the best place to work and learn how to find money for college was in the financial aid office. After two years at Talladega College, I landed an internship with Equitable Life in New York City at 1285 Avenue of the Americas. When the culture shock of that New York summer experience ended, I returned to Talladega College and continued working odd jobs on campus until I graduated. After graduation, I was offered a full-time job at Equitable Life Assurance. I accepted, moved back to New York, and worked in the company's IT department for almost two years before I landed a job in the IT department at PepsiCo in White Plains, New York (Westchester County). I worked for PepsiCo for about twelve years before I accepted a transfer to a different PepsiCo division, Frito-Lay in Plano, Texas. I was with Frito-Lay for about six years before I founded my company, DPLOYIT Staffing, which turned sixteen years old in 2018. I have been legitimately working for money for almost 90 percent of my life.

One day in the summer of 2018, I was sitting in my home office in Plano with my back to the window that faced the front of my house. I heard a vehicle pull up. My curiosity was sparked, so I turned to see what was going on. I immediately noticed a Hispanic-looking man get out of the driver's side of a pickup truck that had a trailer attached to it with a couple of lawnmowers and other lawn servicing equipment in it. The man moved quickly to the back of the truck and pulled one of the Weed Eaters off a rack attached to the trailer. After starting the Weed Eater up with just two pulls of the cord, he started to groom the edges of my neighbor's front yard. A few seconds later, a woman walked around the truck from the passenger side. She, too, looked Hispanic. I assumed she was the man's wife. She unlatched and pulled down the gate (which was attached to the trailer) to the point where it touched the street, creating a short ramp to the trailer. She walked up the ramp, grabbed the handle of one of the lawnmowers, carefully backed the mower down the ramp, and pushed the mower over the curb and onto the sidewalk. The woman leaned over and pulled the cord with all her might, and the lawnmower started up on the second pull. Without hesitating, the woman started to mow the front yard of my neighbor's house. She continued pushing the mower back and forth across the lawn as her husband continued with his own craft—smoothly managing the Weed Eater to trim the edges of the lawn. After watching the synchronized dance for several minutes, without equivocating, I sat back in my seat and subconsciously thought to myself, *How might that conversation have gone in families of other races?* I had to be honest, I was especially deliberating how that conversation would have unfolded in a Black American family or a white American family when the husband-wife couple were in the planning stage of the business. The point here is simple. All citizens (adults and children) who plan to enjoy their inalienable right to "pursue" happiness in this country must be willing to do whatever it takes to legally earn money. Full stop!

The Fair Labor Standards Act prohibits children from working if they are under fourteen years of age. In addition, the law limits the number of hours they can work if they are fewer than sixteen years of age. Teenagers over the age of sixteen can work full-time jobs. However, if the teen is under the age of eighteen, he or she is not allowed to work more than eight hours per day nor more than forty hours per week. Starting at age eighteen, one can work full-time and overtime. State laws have different guidelines for child labor.

With all that said, I'd like to put into perspective the value of work, ironically related to free labor. Slaves were forced to work for free. They were not compensated for the free labor they provided in the process of building the United States' foundational economy. To put this into perspective, some estimates suggest free slave labor in the United States would equal, in today's dollar value, more than $20 trillion.

Parents

It is critically important that every child hone a solid and grounded work ethic. Parents unwilling to take charge of basic and fundamental accountability must teach their children that neglecting the profound importance and value of working will ultimately be complicit in the children's eventual struggles, which might yield marginal to no success. Children who miss the point or fail to appreciate the value of working early in their young lives will suffer severe consequences later in life.

In many cases, the basis for parents neglecting their responsibility to sharpen their children's will to work is grounded in the fact that many of us never got it right ourselves. By never themselves learning the value of working, our parents may have missed the opportunity to appropriately teach us. On the other hand, some parents are unwilling or lack the courage to step up and do what's required to be developed for the different levels of suitable jobs. This reality makes it hard to guide children and others.

The following represents a short list of the primary categories of jobs available for children before they can be hired in legitimate jobs. These are the jobs that parents get to leverage as a way to teach their children the value of working.

Consider these categories:

- **Premature work:** Children need to understand very early in life that they will always have to work for what they earn. In addition, they will need to establish some level of what they perceive to be their personal value.
- **Accountable work:** There will always be tasks to be done that are required for children to simply take good care of themselves, their living environment, others (like grandparents), and the pets within their realm. Children should not be compensated for that level of accountable work.

Parents should leverage premature work to teach their children the value of working while they are still too young to legally work for money. It's important for children to learn to appreciate that they will eventually have to work to sustain a living. Moreover, children must learn to understand the value of the work they do. In this regard, children should be taught to expect compensation or pay for work.

A good example of premature work is when a child is asked by his father to help with grooming the lawn on Saturday morning. Parents could also establish a weekly task for their child to complete, like vacuuming the carpet on Saturdays. This is the kind of premature work parents might consider compensating their child for—maybe in the form of an allowance. However, to ensure a "teachable moment" or experience, there should be a definitive connection between the work and the payment for the work completed. Parents must not miss this point. When premature work is taught and executed in the right context, your child will grow to be eager to work around the house and complete chores for extra money.

Premature work is also a good way to create situational bonding opportunities between the parent and the child. Imagine having a mature conversation with your child while they learn valuable lessons like how to use a paint roller or mow the lawn for the first time. There are many ways to achieve dual value with your children during teachable moments and bonding.

Finally, it would be a disservice to teach a child how to earn money and not teach the child the value of giving help to others who may be less fortunate. Parents also have an accountability to teach their children the importance of saving and the related discipline required to build wealth.

Parents must be careful not to compensate children for completing accountable work—everyday tasks that a child should be expected to do. These tasks should not be eligible for allowance. Some work is just expected of a child as part of the child's responsibility—for instance, the work a child does in the process of correcting a mess they were responsible for creating (e.g., tidying up his or her room). There will always be a delicate balance between accountable work and premature work. In fact, there are lessons you can use to teach your child about each.

Children

Understanding the different types of work will be key to children reaching a decision in terms of the job or career they choose. While having a college degree is not necessary (but highly recommended) to land a well-paying job, children have a broad range of career options.

The following short list is intended to put different levels of jobs into perspective:

Blue-collar work, in simple terms, is honorable and honest. In fact, most jobs in the US job market are blue-collar jobs. While blue-collar work is often linked to hard labor, many US citizens take pride in mastering certain skills and crafts for the purpose of providing a living and a lifestyle for their family. Blue-collar work may include lifting heavy items, completing repetitive tasks, working outside, assembling parts in warehouses, etc. Blue-collar work also includes working in a restaurant, serving food, and waiting tables. Nonetheless, blue-collar workers represent the financial backbone of the most critical aspect of the US economy—consumers.

My philosophy is simple. Children should enter the workforce as soon as they are old enough to do so. They will be shocked to learn about the taxes they are required to pay once tax season rolls around. Parents can include a crash course for their children on this recurring liability. You see, parents don't usually take taxes out of allowance money. In any case, blue-collar work is usually the way young teenagers are introduced into the US workforce.

Independent contractor work can be very lucrative. While a college degree may prove to be of value to the individual who chooses to offer services independently, it is not always necessary. Education aside, a contractor must be best in class in their trade. My company has staffed individuals who were highly skilled in SAP technology and internet security. At least one independent contractor who was assigned to one of our Fortune company clients was compensated $500 per hour. While that example represents the outlier for an independent contractor, I think my point is clear. When individuals are willing to hone certain skills known to be in very high demand in the workforce, they can become the go-to contractor for key and unique niche work—the kind of work major companies are willing to pay big bucks for.

On the other hand, there are independent contractors who simply paint homes and interiors extremely well and demand top dollar for their services. The certified electrician who completed the work in my garage was an independent contractor who charged $80.00 per hour. In addition, the man and woman who mow my neighbor's lawn are—more than likely—independent contractors. Housekeepers are independent contractors as well. Therefore, when I consider independent contractor work, I'm compelled to believe there is absolutely no good reason why a healthy man or woman should not be working.

Entrepreneurial work is related to individuals or teams of individuals willing to work for themselves in a more structured business model than working as an individual or independent contractor. My friend Fern Johnson invited me to her home to hear a business pitch from a young man named James. James was graduating from high school in a few days, was planning to go to college, and was keenly focused on starting a business in the gaming industry with two of his close friends. James led the presentation and pitch to this group of very successful executives who were currently in key middle-management and senior-management roles at different Fortune companies. Each of James's friends got to participate in the presentation as well. I was impressed. These young men were crisp in terms of their structured delivery, they spoke very well, and made their points very clear. It was obvious they had done some research on the gaming industry related to their business concept. The young men were knowledgeable about market trends and specifically up to date on recent trends in the markets of Plano, Texas, and neighboring Frisco. In the end, James indicated, based on their projections, they would be seeking investments of close to $200,000.

When the trio finished their presentation, they opened the floor for questions. As I led the tough question-and-answer session, the audience learned that the young men had not actually started a business by registering it with a US state. They did not have a bank account. They did not have a business plan. They did not have an Employer Identification Number (EIN), which is applied for and issued by the IRS. They did not clearly understand profit and loss. They did not understand the concept of a balance sheet or equity. They did not understand the consequences of "comingling" funds between their personal bank accounts and the business accounts. The question-and-answer session was not intended to denigrate James and his team. The point was to make it clear to them and any teenager reading this book that you must have your ducks in a row regarding the small business you've started or are planning to start—before you start doing business, and definitely before you start inviting investors into your realm.

Entrepreneur businesses can grow into major companies with thousands of employees. It's a great way to get on a path to becoming affluent. Keep in mind, entrepreneurship includes investing in franchises like McDonalds or Chick-fil-A.

However, one of the hottest opportunities available right now is in the field of logistics—the profession of analyzing and meeting the demands of consumers.

Internships are the best on-the-job training a teenager can experience—especially if you're planning to work in corporate America. You can gain insight into what it's like to work in corporate jobs, midrange businesses, or small businesses. Internships are important because the work you do will in some way be connected to the actual business of the company you work for.

While interning at Equitable Life Assurance Company, I was responsible for configuring dialup modems that were used for retrieving sales information from remote satellite offices around the country. Although I had done some coding in college, I had not worked on the telecommunications side of IT before. But think about it: I was just nineteen years old and responsible for retrieving—via telecommunications—millions of dollars in sales data for a major Fortune company. Imagine if I had somehow corrupted the data or lost it. There would have been a good chance I would not have been invited back to work at Equitable Life Assurance.

College students should start securing internships with companies as freshmen. If your area of focus is in marketing and you have your eye set on landing a job with major Fortune companies like PepsiCo, you need to be ready. Firstly, a lot of the Fortune giants, especially ones with funny ads in the Super Bowl, will expect prospective candidates to have a minimum of two or three internships listed in their credentials. Secondly, to land a full-time role at one of these major companies, a master's degree in marketing may be required. Each college graduate must plan to complete three internships while in college. Your goal should be to complete a minimum of two internships. Students who graduate with fewer than two internships under their belts will find themselves at a competitive disadvantage to other students who treat internships more seriously.

White-collar work is primarily work in the corporate offices of major Fortune companies and any company where professional work is managed. This level of work does not require employees to lift heavy items or perform any of the work described in the blue-collar work section. White-collar workers are usually professional workers and managers with college degrees and solid work experience. These jobs include titles like analyst, business analyst, financial analyst, manager, and director.

Employees who work in white-collar jobs are usually paid salaries—a fixed pay rate—regardless of the hours they work. While overtime is not allowed or compensated for, there are other perks that make white-collar jobs very attractive, such as vacation time off, sick time off, health insurance, life insurance, stock options, promotions, bonus pay, and other perks.

In the past, corporate work cultures required employees to wear suits and ties to work. I never completely understood that cultural norm, but I followed the rules. Today, however, those rules have changed. It seems no one, including CEOs and other executives, wear ties. In fact, these days there is flex time, meaning employees can come to work late and leave later as a way to accommodate their family schedules and plans. Some employees work from home. As long as your work is done, where you do it is not as important any more. Millennials have and are driving a lot of the corporate culture change—so much so that Google has cots in its open lobby that young millennials use to take afternoon naps while at work.

White-collar work is like an internship on steroids as white-collar employees' work accountabilities are more closely connected to the company's actual business. When I was working at PepsiCo managing multi-million-dollar national projects, I required each member on my teams to take commutes with the Pepsi and Frito-Lay sales teams responsible for generating revenue for the beverage and snack food giants. While we all worked in the IT department, I thought it was important for my staff to understand the intricacies of PepsiCo's business. I also strongly suggested they take tours of the manufacturing facilities so that they would gain a full understanding of the millions of dollars per hour in productivity that could be lost if the technology we were building and supporting was to experience a catastrophic failure.

Executive work is the level of corporate work where the big bucks are made in terms of salaries, stock options, and bonuses. As such, there are fewer of these jobs to be had. These jobs include senior directors, vice presidents, senior vice presidents, executive vice presidents, presidents, and chief executive officers like Ken Chenault, former CEO of American Express, who just happens to be Black American. I decided to feature Chenault because I have a firm belief that just as President Barack Obama became president of the United States, each teen reading this book can become president of the United States or CEO of a Fortune 500 company, like Ken Chenault. It simply depends on what you're willing to do to get there. To put executive work into perspective, some of the most highly compensated CEOs made over $100,000,000 as their total compensation package in 2018.

Sports work is a possible avenue of work. However, to make good money, you must become an executive on a college or professional team or play as a professional athlete. The number of jobs available in this industry is very limited, and only the students who are considered or proven to be best in class will be eligible to fill the few jobs available during each annual draft cycle. It should also be noted that all of the major sports organizations hire summer interns in areas such as marketing, finance, IT, operations, supply chain, and so on. Certainly, some of these jobs would be cool to land.

12

Integrity

A person's integrity is measured by the combination of their inner qualities and their outward behaviors. The true measure, in simple terms, is based on what you do and how you do it. These measurements are usually related to how people behave and how others perceive their behavior. Your integrity will be valued based on how you cause others to feel about you or view you, determined in part by how they assess your values. This level of judgment will often be completely outside your control. However, because your integrity is so critical to your life, the way in which you carry yourself and your style will be important in influencing people to perceive you in a positive light.

Make sure your heart is in the right place most of the time and that you are presenting yourself with good behavior. People must try as best they can to be good and genuine in their deeds. Fairness is also a measure of integrity. Keep in mind that people are hearing what you say. They are aware of your movement and your style. People notice how you treat others. They notice how you speak, what you wear, and how you wear it. People use your outward presentation of yourself to measure who they perceive you to be.

Merriam-Webster's defines "integrity" as "firm adherence to a code of especially moral or artistic values—incorruptibility." Integrity is always characterized by the good and varying levels of quality in a person. Integrity is often used to describe strength as the fitness of foundations and physical structures, such as buildings. However, as it relates to people, integrity, for the most part, is considered in terms of a person's inner qualities and strengths together with how they present themselves outwardly. Integrity in individuals is first derived from within—intrinsic qualities developed over a lifetime. It is always fluid, as it is shaped and reshaped over time based on individuals' life experiences. It is not possible for a person to have bad integrity because the measure of integrity is always represented by good characteristics and qualities.

Integrity is presented fundamentally based on the internal choices individuals make that drive their behaviors and the physical actions they publicly present. However, the outcome of the choices is always used to measure integrity. Your integrity is what keeps you grounded and legitimate in the eyes of others within and without your realm. Integrity has the power to command trust and respect from others—including random strangers. On the other hand, questionable integrity yields an opposite effect on people in terms of the way they view and treat you.

Generally, citizens assign high marks to the integrity of police officers around the country. The few times I've witnessed white police officers genuinely stop their patrol cars to play a little basketball with the young Black children in the neighborhood sent powerful messages to me regarding those officer's integrity. However, when I witness time and time again white police officers on camera shooting first with deadly force and killing unarmed Black men and boys, the experience causes me to question the entire workforce of police officers' integrity. I question: Is there something systemic about that?

Over the course of my life I've learned that if your integrity is not in check, not much else matters. Integrity has a lot to do with trust. You can be the richest man or woman in the world, but if your values are questioned and your ethics are out of alignment with good qualities, you can still lose it all. The rules, in this regard, do not always apply equally to all citizens. People of color should be highly cognizant of controlling how others view and perceive us—especially our children. For instance, if you make a choice to wear your pants hanging off your butt, people will look at you and treat you like your pants are hanging off your butt. There is a good chance you will not be taken seriously.

But, more important than that, the use of the n-word to describe another human being is irresponsible and lacks integrity and anything associated with it. The word is demeaning and has always been intended to belittle Black American men and disrespect the entire race of Black American people. The n-word is not a term of endearment. Using it in any way—especially in public—will, without question, diminish a person's respect and integrity.

The issue I have with integrity is that it can only be judged and responded to by people—random people. Integrity is what it is. However, when ordinary people make conscious choices to ignore your true values and respond to you in a way counter to who you really are, this can be a major problem. In this regard, people get it wrong. In fact, they sometimes intentionally get it wrong based on the person being judged. But that is just how our culture has been conditioned. Factions of us have been shaped into beliefs about stereotypes and bad impressions—the kinds of stereotypes and impressions that people allow to outweigh or overlook a person's true values, intentions, and integrity. For instance, these kinds of issues are embedded in certain people's belief that another group of people is better or that all people in a race group are racist—neither of which is true. Nonetheless, these are the values and beliefs that linger and contribute to the divisiveness that haunts our culture and serves as the basis for cultural profiling, police brutality, and a persisting divided society.

Every person's life will forever be shaped by the choices they make—especially adults. People's expectations and measurements of integrity are different for children, adolescents, and adults. Because integrity is essentially measured by others within your realm, you should be cognizant of where you are and who's watching or listening. Choices may not always be the basis for the trouble you find yourself in. The basis is usually linked to the outcome of your choice. For instance, a man who robs a bank and never gets caught will not necessarily experience any consequences for his actions. However, when he is caught, the consequences will be life changing.

It is unfortunate that in these current times it is still necessary to remind the citizenry of our country that Black Americans are being forced to exist under a different brand of citizenship than whites and people of other races.

Nonetheless, this is the reality. For Black Americans to ignore this fact would be remiss and possibly fatal. It is important for me to press this issue because I am profoundly concerned about Black American men and boys. In fact, I am sometimes concerned about my own life being shortened because of my skin color and certain random encounters with the wrong people. I am concerned because it is a proven fact that even when Black Americans are idle or making all the right choices, they are still treated differently, punished more harshly, and sometimes (way too many times) killed. Therefore, I am compelled to remind our young Black boys and men about these unique circumstances so that they will have fair chances to conform, which will contribute to somehow prolonging their lives. In fact, we must do more than just remind these young, promising men; we must teach them.

Despite these unique situations, Black Americans must continue to enhance their collective integrity with nonviolence while continuing to compete for equality with intellectual tactics. Since being freed from slavery, Black Americans have suffered hardship for more than one hundred and fifty years. However, there are no legitimate excuses for Black American unaccountability. Black Americans own the accountability to change their predicaments; no one else can change them for us. That is exactly what your integrity is all about—your accountability for yourself and others within your realm and your respect for who you are and where you have come from. Furthermore, Black Americans are free enough to take charge of and own the change we long for. Black Americans must establish the collective will to ensure our children are equipped with the level of intellect required to ensure a new era by the 2060s. To achieve such a monumental feat, Black American children's integrity must be groomed and intact. It may take another fifty years, but imagine two million Black American children all grown up. Now imagine them working and with families. Imagine these children with solid integrity, good intensions, and high intelligence. Imagine them with solid social, business, and political relationships. Finally, imagine these children driving the change by bringing other children of all races along. The whole world will have changed.

When I was manager in the IT department at PepsiCo in Somers, New York, I attended an orientation meeting with the new summer interns.

Lawrence Jackson, a very senior-level Black American executive at PepsiCo, was the keynote speaker. Near the end of his speech, as he was covering the topic of integrity, he unexpectedly exclaimed, "You see—most people at PepsiCo don't get fired because they are incompetent. PepsiCo hires very qualified people." He continued, "Most people get fired because they do stupid s***!"

He went on to talk about how employees misuse the travel expense report process by including non-business-related items (such as personal expenses) on their expense reports. Before moving on, Jackson offered a few more examples of questionable integrity before he closed out his speech. Less than a year later, a close friend of mine was terminated from her six-figure job for misusing her expense report. The reality is that you never want to have people question your integrity, especially people who trust and respect you, such as your employer, your parents, a close friend, or anyone you consider a friend, a business partner, a mentor, or family members. The consequences of questionable integrity can be disastrous and life changing.

Today, the way most parents teach their children about the importance of ensuring that they understand right from wrong is not so different than it was in the 1960s. However, consequently, far too many parents still punish their children by spanking them with belts, switches, branches, and (yes) extension cords on their bare skin. It's unfortunate because each time a child is treated that way, the child is taught a lesson about how they should treat their own children when they're older. It's a sad but true reality—indicative of how these norms are passed down for generations. But while spanking your child may not be intended to have them pass the norm forward, spankings still serve as lessons to a child. Therefore, unless this norm of harshly punishing children is somehow corrected, children will carry the experience with them for the rest of their lives.

Intentionally or not, parents don't always teach their children the right things or instill in them what most people would consider the best values. Some parents intentionally teach their children values counter to popular ones and counter to United States' stated values: racism, notions of superiority, the use of the n-word, and inspiring children to make colloquial idioms and dialects a priority over the requirement to learn and speak English. This happens to be one of my most profound pet peeves. I believe any parent, regardless of race, who intentionally denies a child the opportunity to speak the English language—the absolute basis for achieving in our country—is fundamentally wrong, and the action should be punishable under US law. It should be considered child abuse, with severe consequences—including fines but not limited to arrest and imprisonment.

Nonetheless, because all parents aren't perfect, it is important for children, as they grow older, to play significant roles in shaping their own values—their own integrity. That is exactly what this chapter is about. In fact, that is exactly what this entire book is about: children at some point owning their integrity so they have the right and accountability to nurture and shape it based on their knowledge and their personal, intrinsic values. This notion comes with a tipping point—a decision as to whether a child will consciously choose to or be forced to go against the grain, and in some cases against their parents' teachings. For instance, in cases where their parents' teachings don't necessarily align with their values, children will have to muster up the courage to stand for what they view as fundamentally right. This reality will be crucial as we head into the 2060s.

To have a strong and foundational integrity, you must first establish a value system, know exactly what your values are, be able to recognize when your values are being compromised, and respond accordingly. Integrity has two of the WIN life principles:

1. Accountability: An action value that has as its basis the will of a person related to the good and poor choices they make—choices people are required to account for.
2. Respect: A judgment value associated with how people view your qualities or values and the way you treat others. It's important to have respect for yourself. It is equally important to respect others.

13

Integrity Life Principle: Accountability

For a long time, I struggled to put accountability into context. I previously said I measured the value of accountability over the value of hope. Then I changed my mind. Hope is more powerful because it inspires accountability.

Our children need to be taught a great deal about their individual accountability. The earlier they know and understand the things for which they will be held accountable, the better. They need answers so they can be equipped with the knowledge to make informed and smart choices. But it is impossible to cover all the data points required to be transmitted to our children in a single setting, conversation, or a book. Consequently, many of our children will be forced to live phases of their lives by chance. Inevitably, some of them will fail and learn the hard way from their mishaps and mistakes. Therefore, the goal should be to proactively mitigate those kinds of incidents. The best way to do that is to fully understand your child's potential and work hard to enhance your child's chances for succeeding.

Like most people, my personal journey has been all over the place and fraught with surprises—surprises that forced me to make spontaneous choices: the worse kinds of choices, and the kind children can only hope they get right.

The common incidents that made or broke me—and ultimately shaped my life—have been linked to the choices I made. I have made smart choices in my life. I have great stories to tell people and children about my life's journey; moreover, I have advice to offer related to directions they should take or what they should do or at least consider doing. In addition, because I have been forced to deal with the outcomes of some really bad choices I've made, I have a lot to say about the kinds of things and activities people should shy away from and never do in their lives. My life has taught me that individual accountability weighs heavily on the choices people make over a lifetime.

Parents must accept the fact that, at some point, their children will be forced to follow their own intuition and make smart choices on their own. The key point here is that children's intuition is shaped by the teachings of their parents. The role parents play is far more important than most parents understand. If they understood their role better, they would very aggressively shape their children's integrity by ensuring their foundational values are aligned with faith, hope, peace, equality, respect, and good will. I could add more values here, but the point is clear.

With their parents' guidance, children must be accountable for taking charge of every aspect of their lives as early as possible. They must be held accountable for their life, their liberty, and their purposeful pursuit of some level of happiness. Forget all the complexity; it's as simple as that.

Perspective

Knowing that we are endowed by our Creator with certain inalienable rights, we have a responsibility to call out the absolute farce this is for too many in our society. We must live up to our precepts as a society for all citizens. The United States is one of the most unforgiving countries in the entire world—unforgiving of its citizens who get caught up in the penal system. In this country, being unaccountable could be life changing because a single bad choice could dictate how and where you will live the rest of your life. The most common punishment is incarceration. However, in many states, it is legal for federal and local penal systems to take your life.

The US population represents approximately 4 percent of the world population, whereas people incarcerated in the US represent 25 percent of people incarcerated in the entire world. Being incarcerated is the absolute worst thing to impart on your existence. The US prison system is not conducive to real rehabilitation. You will find yourself fighting for your life regularly, which means you could potentially have more time added onto your sentence. Moreover, the aftermath of your imprisonment could be worse than being locked up. You will lose your right to vote. Finding a job with a felony record will be close to impossible. If you are released on parole or probation, any slight infraction could land you back in jail or in prison—caught up in a recidivism nightmare, as close to 76 percent of inmates return to state prisons and 44 percent of federal inmates return to prison within five years. The answer to this problem is very simple—stay out of trouble. As my mother would say, "Boy—you know better!" Be accountable for your choices because it will be impossible to pursue happiness if you are dead or incarcerated.

Parents

Children are taught early in their lives to behave. However, it is virtually impossible to teach children everything there is to know about life and appropriate behaviors while they are young. In this regard, children are allowed certain exceptions related to bad behavior. Teenagers—not so much. Adults—not at all.

My mother taught my siblings and me about good and bad behavior early and often. If we were within the confines of our home, she had an internal threshold associated with how long she would wait to discipline me when I got out of line. However, when we were in public, the rules completely changed. For instance, when we were visiting her friends the Graggs, who lived on the other side of town, we knew we had to behave. If I even tested the waters with any level of bad behavior by playing around too much—especially if I knocked something over or came close to doing so—that meant trouble. My mother would grab me by the arm, pull me to a nearby corner away from the rest of the group, lean over with her face almost touching mine, and, with clenched teeth, say to me forcefully and in a voice that started out as a whisper and ended as a roar, "Boy, you better act like you've been somewhere before!" Her message was very clear. That was all it took to motivate my siblings and me to sit our butts down somewhere. We knew if she had to tell us again, there would be consequences. It wasn't necessarily the way she had instructed us to settle down. It was more what we all knew would come next if we got out of bounds with our behavior in the company of her friends. It was the norm in our community. While we didn't have much, we were taught to behave. More than likely, our parents did not want any of us to have to face "the law," as they called the police.

Back in those days, Black Americans in our neighborhood used the word "civilized" often to describe how we should behave—especially in terms of our behavior in public. It was their way of teaching us right from wrong and, in the process, shaping our integrity in the early years of our lives.

Parents own the accountability to tell their children the truth about the potential outcomes of good and bad choices. For instance, one of the absolute worst things a parent can do to their child is to allow their child to steal or take something that does not belong to them without seizing the opportunity for a teachable moment.

In some cases, adolescents will enjoy the benefit of exceptions. Because they are not considered intellectually capable of making responsible choices, they will get free passes for some of the bad choices they make. However, there is a very thin line between the exceptions and the young men and young women who will be inevitably forced to learn things the hard way via trial and error. Therefore, it is critically important for young teens to get the integrity thing right the first time and for the rest of their lives. When teenagers fall short of this very important responsibility, the consequences can be life changing. For example, because of certain bad choices made by young teenagers or adolescents, our penal system prescribes that teens be charged for certain crimes as adults. Therefore, if a teenager makes a misstep, that young person could be locked up for the majority of his or her life.

Most adults know right from wrong. We should know better. Nonetheless, adults are the ones who knowingly and purposefully make poor choices—including choices with significant risks attached. This level of ignorance may set the worst examples for your children. The fact is—luck runs out, and a life or a few lives could be forever changed.

Going forward, parents who teach their child that they are better than children of other race groups because they are white will do so at their child's peril. Moreover, at some point, the child will be faced with making the choice as to whether they will continue to cling to and carry forward such beliefs into the future and toward the 2060s. Parents who teach children values of white privilege but miss the opportunity to ensure their children are accountable for developing the skills required in the workforce will be complicit in their children's marginal success and related poverty. Furthermore, the parent who thinks speaking proper English will make the child sound too white will be fully complicit in sabotaging their child's education, their ability to build relationships, their questionable integrity, and their ability to command respect.

Parents aren't perfect. As I have mentioned throughout this book, children and young teenagers will ultimately own the accountability to make the right choices regarding these kinds of teachings. In fact, children will eventually arrive at decisions that may be counter to their parents' teachings—decisions linked to values worthy or not of being taught to their children as we forge ahead to the 2060s.

Children

As a teenager, the accountability for your choices will be shifted from your parents to you. With this new responsibility, you must take it seriously because your life may depend on how responsible you can be.

My mother, Catherine Harper, had an uncanny way of reminding her ten children she was our mother. She would simply say, "I brought you into the world, and I will take you out!" Many parents in the South treated their children that way. It was a tactic designed to ensure we behaved in hopes of our never being taken away by the police. But she never took us out. Yes—she said it, but she never did it. There was no way she would. She loved my nine siblings and me too much. She was a serious Catholic with strong values. Despite the racism, she never taught us to hate anyone. She told us that we would have to be "ten times better" and work "twice as hard."

Once, when I was around seven years old, I was with my mother and a few of my other siblings in the grocery store. I saw a little girl and told my mother, "She's ugly."

My mother immediately removed her right hand from the shopping cart, slapped me on my arm really hard, and responded, "Don't say that about people." She continued, "You know better, Ralph . . . That's somebody's child."

When I was free from my mother's control for the first time, I was mindful that I literally had the right to do whatever I wanted to do that night—even if she found out about it. Thanks to my mother, the experience was a little frightening for me. Even though I had graduated from the brief era of spankings, I was still afraid of doing anything to disappoint her. That is the kind of power she imposed on my siblings and me. That is the level of protection she willed upon her children. That is the level of love and care with which she nurtured us. These are the values that shaped and saved our lives in a time in the South when grown men and women were vulnerable to systemic differences.

Although I know all parents are not created equal, children's first accountability should be to love, honor, support, and protect their parents. Beyond that, teenagers must be prepared to be accountable for their own life, liberty, and pursuit of happiness.

Life

Teenagers own the accountability to maintain their bodies and their lives. Even if children aren't athletic or planning to be athletes, they must be conscious of their health. I imagine many children think because they are young they can't get sick. Meanwhile, children and teenagers are diagnosed with illnesses like diabetes, heart conditions, and cancers every single day. I make this point because the earlier illnesses and diseases are discovered, the more likely it will be that they can be treated and a child's life potentially saved.

A huge mistake teens make is discovering the short-term intoxication of alcohol and drugs. Most teens are not responsible enough to drink. In addition, peer pressure is one of the main reasons teen drinkers go overboard. Fraternities use alcohol to haze neophytes. In some cases, these practices have resulted in the death of young students, and the young student perpetrators' lives have been forever changed. Beyond the fun of drinking lies a serious problem with alcohol addictions, which may lead to other kinds of addictions like heroin usage. For these reasons, teenagers must be very aware of life and living. Too many children have met their fates much too soon, losing their lives in accidents and overdosing. "The rate of teen drug overdose deaths in the United States climbed 19% from 2014 to 2015, from 3.1 deaths per 100,000 teens to 3.7 per 100,000," according to the CNN report "Teen Drug Overdose Death Rate Climbed 19% in one Year" by Nadia Kounang (August 16, 2017, https://www.cnn.com/2017/08/16/health/teen-overdose-death-rate/index.html). Heroin overdoses were the primary cause of these deaths.

According to a report by the parent resource program, Youth Suicide Statistics, "more teenagers and young adults die from suicide than from cancer, heart disease, AIDS, birth defects, stroke, pneumonia, influenza, and chronic lung disease, combined."

In addition to the aforementioned data points, Black American children have a unique accountability to appropriately respond to their encounters with law enforcement officers. Given the racial climate in our country related to the disparity of Black men and boys killed by white cops, it makes absolute sense to set your pride aside to ensure you survive simple encounters with police. This is not to suggest every white police officer is crooked. However, because of who you are, the facts suggest you could be at risk, so always be cautious and respectful.

Seemingly to contribute to systemic plans to stoke police brutality, there has been an increase in the number of white people calling the police on law-abiding Black Americans. It's the new way of creating intentional police confrontations with Black Americans. It happened in a Starbucks store in Philadelphia. It happened in a park in California where Blacks were legally barbecuing when a white woman called the police. It happened to a friend, Johnny Wimbrey, a celebrity international speaker, teacher, and writer in my hometown of Plano, Texas. Johnny had been seated at Sambuca Restaurant and was about to have dinner with his wife when the white manager came over and asked him to give up his seat to another white patron who happened to be a regular. After my friend declined and started recording the experience, the white Sambuca manger called the cops and tried making false statements regarding Johnny's behavior during the incident. These are the kinds of encounters that end with Black American men becoming victims of deadly force.

Pride or Die

Throughout this book, I have noted that Black Americans exist under a different brand of citizenship than any other citizen group. There are several factually supported realities that serve as proof of the unique situation Black Americans find themselves in here. This reality is most evident in the US judicial system.

Tips—Pride or Die

- *Do not* run from a police officer.
- Respect the authority of all police officers.
- Refer to the police officer as "sir" or "ma'am" or "officer."
- Follow the instructions of all police officers—no deviations.
- When the police officer asks questions, answer with respect, and speak very clearly.
- If it's not too late, *do not* keep your phone in your hand.
- *Do not* attempt to put your phone away when the police officer is approaching you and has you in plain sight.
- Only if you are in your car, if you decide to record the policing encounter, start the recording prior to the police officer reaching your vehicle, and leave the phone on the seat or center console.
- If you have a gun or any weapon on your person or in your car, tell the police officer about the weapon and where it is located. *Do not* reach for the weapon or make any abrupt move to show the weapon to the officer.
- Always keep your hands where they can be clearly seen by the officer—even if it means raising them above your head.
- If you are in your car, place your hands on the steering wheel in the ten and two positions.
- *Do not* abruptly get out of your car.
- *Do not* use profanity during any encounter with a police officer. Keep your attitude in check.

- If you are placed under arrest (even if you believe there is no cause), *do not* resist arrest or complain or say anything. Set your pride aside so that you can survive each policing encounter.

Liberty

Freedom is not guaranteed—especially for certain race groups. In fact, some of us are required to work harder than others to preserve or secure freedom. That's just the way it is. Our children need to clearly understand these realities early in their lives so that they are equipped with the knowledge to make the kinds of choices that could mitigate any chance of them experiencing the US penal system. Although my voice has not always had the reach or warranted echoes by others who believe in my views, I've spent a large part of my life writing and sending clear messages to children and adults regarding their accountability to be free. In fact, when I was in college and student president of Talladega College's business organization, I took a group of business students on a bus tour just over an hour or so to Atlanta, Georgia. We visited the Peachtree Plaza, a General Motors plant, and the local jail. It was my and our dean's intent to expose our students to a few career and life options.

The experience of sustained liberty is mostly based on an individual's actions related to the choices they make. A bad choice is not always about the actual choice. Your entire life could depend on the outcome of the choice.

Consider the young man who decides to ship illegal drugs from Miami to a friend in New York. Everything goes well. The package is delivered, and the friend confirms the delivery. Now, because the young man was successful shipping drugs without any incident, he might be inspired to try it again. So, he gives it a shot. He follows the same procedure, uses the exact same shipping material and packaging, and ships from the exact same post office he previously used. He waits in line, determined to have the exact same person who assisted him with shipping the previous package assist again. As the new package is in the delivery process and on its journey to New York, a police dog in Tennessee sniffs out the package, thereby identifying it as suspicious. Later, the man who shipped the package is visited by the local police in Miami. He's arrested, tried in a court of law, convicted, and sentenced to five years in prison—the outcome of a very bad choice. This single poor choice could prove to be the destruction of a person's entire life, especially for Black Americans.

Nonetheless, incarceration robs you not only of your freedom but of your dignity and all but one of your inalienable rights—life. While a person is incarcerated, their actions will be dictated by the guardsmen in charge of overseeing them. Guards will tell you when you eat and when you can leave the confinement of your tiny cell. They will tell you when it's OK to go outside to experience the rays of the sun and dictate for how long you can stay. Incarceration equates to very limited access to the outside world. You will not be able to pick up an iPhone or any phone to call a family member. Your privacy will be limited, and you may have no choice but to relieve yourself in front of another cellmate. You will, in many cases, have a roommate who sleeps in the bed above or below you. You will have very little or no access to even speak to a person of the opposite sex. Your life will belong to one of the fifty states of the US government.

A significant percentage of the US prison system is privatized. In simple terms, this means that businesses get paid a lot of money to incarcerate US citizens. In this regard, the business owners who will be responsible for the incarceration of our citizens have a vested interest in our citizens being locked up and staying with them (incarcerated) for as long as possible.

One of the easiest things to do while you are incarcerated is to get in trouble. Imagine if you are incarcerated with a person who is serving a life sentence, and you have an encounter with him (i.e., a fight). Your engagement in the encounter could add additional time to your sentence. You could get caught up in a vicious cycle of inmate crime and become a career prisoner.

I recently watched a show on television that, for me, exposed the one form of punishment in the US that is worse than the death penalty—solitary confinement. It was one of those shows like the *Lockup* series on CNN and MSNBC that covers people who are incarcerated in prisons around the country. I witnessed men in very small cells—no more than eight feet by six feet or so. Each cell was occupied by a single inmate. The single door of each cell was firmly locked. A single window in each door may have measured eighteen to twenty inches in length by five inches wide. I do not believe there were windows with views to the outside. Each cell was equipped with a toilet, a sink, and a hard concrete or wooden bed with a thin mattress and a blanket. As I listened to the commentators cover the story of this prison, I was dumbfounded. The guards calmly described how men were locked away for twenty-three hours per day and allowed one hour of freedom to go outside.

I saw grown men crying in their cells—begging for help. I saw at least two prisoners with their faces against the glass window in the doors, licking the glass with their tongues. One prisoner seemed to be trying to bite the glass. Another prisoner was making very weird and scary faces with his eyes rolling around in his head. I could hear moans, groans, and sobbing from other men I could not visibly see on my television. It was one of the most inhumane travesties I have ever witnessed in my life. I wondered what in the hell they could have done to deserve such a level of punishment.

Then I contemplated the casual attitude of the guards responsible for the management of the facility. Some had smiles and smirks on their faces as they explained to the reporter what they were witnessing and why these men were incarcerated. The guards calmly told the reporters how they were required to shackle the inmates prior to escorting them to their one hour of freedom per day. The experience brought tears to my eyes as I questioned the integrity of men with such cold hearts that they were willing to make a living that way. I questioned what it might be like for the guards when they go home each night to sit at the dinner table with their families. I can't imagine. The television experience made it clear to me that I never want to be incarcerated in my life.

I believe all teenagers should visit a prison to gain a clear understanding about integrity and the outcomes of choices. Furthermore, the experience may inspire our youth to be more deliberate in terms of their focus on pursuing happiness. What I am suggesting may be viewed by some as extreme. However, it is important that we go the extra mile to protect our children from themselves and our society. It is important to tell them and expose them to the harsh but true realities of life.

Pursuit of Happiness

To pursue happiness, you must be prepared—prepared to make money. To enjoy happiness, you must follow and live by at least the first five REWARDS life principles (reading, education, work, accountability, and respect). You will have to read routinely and continue reading for the rest of your life. You must be educated formally with a bachelor's degree, master's degree, or doctorate degree. Otherwise, you will have to become an expert in certain skills and disciplines required to run a business, work as an independent contractor, or become a professional speaker. You will have to experience and appreciate the value and need to work. You will have to be respectful of people and command respect from others. You will have to be accountable for your choices as you survive and live. You will have to mitigate all risks of being incarcerated so that you can retain 100 percent of your freedom in the United States.

For most people in this country, the pursuit of happiness is supported by cold hard cash. Happiness is, for the most part, made possible by what a person can afford to do and acquire—assets, services, social engagements, and other intangibles, including the profound intrinsic value of supporting other children and world causes. Therefore, saving money, being financially astute, and building and sustaining wealth are necessary.

But while it helps a whole lot, money is not the only way to pursue happiness. The Bible states, "For the love of money is the root of all evil." That is arguably true. On the other hand, based on the choices of people, money can serve for the good of helping others who are less fortunate. That's the way life should be in our country, as there is no value in hoarding money.

A person's happiness will always be relative to the individual's life and their will to pursue their dreams or whatever it is that makes them happy. Some people are very happy knowing they have billions of dollars sitting in the bank and accruing additional wealth every single day via interest rates and other investments. However, considering current and anticipated world calamities like starvation, global warming, and threats of nuclear war, I am not so sure of the value of our wealthiest citizens sitting on the trillions they and their descendants will never be able to spend. I think idle money should also be functional in terms of helping the society we live in.

Anyway, others are content with knowing they are using or have used their wealth to support underserved children, children with cancer, or some of the poorest nations in Africa.

Happiness for others lies somewhere between the happiness of the wealthiest citizens and the intrinsic happiness of the successful philanthropist helping one child at a time. Nonetheless, each citizen gets to determine their standing in terms of the pursuit of their own happiness.

On the journey to pursuing happiness, children should start early in understanding what their happiness will cost. If their goal is to be comfortable living from paycheck to paycheck while saving enough money to retire, there will be little financial flexibility left to support children of the next generation, which I personally believe should be a firm accountability of every child growing up today and forging ahead to the 2060s. The person willing to help others will always be graded and labeled as having high integrity.

Imagine if all our children had opportunities to witness the power of building wealth. Some of the best examples are taught and passed down by parents. However, not all parents have the best examples to share with their children. More parents than not grow up as I did, with very little and limited disposable funds. Just as I did, they learned the hard way. This is another reason it's important for all parents to do as best they can to ensure their children are, at minimum, equipped with the will and skills to achieve more success than they did. However, in the end, there is only one way for the goal of pursuing happiness to be achieved—children own the accountability to make it happen. Therefore, I am asking parents to help guide their children in their pursuits. Moreover, I am asking children to own these accountabilities; hold on to the kinds of values delineated in each set of the REWARDS life principles, and never let go.

In or around 2010, Warren Buffet and Melinda and Bill Gates started an initiative where the two families pledged to give more than 50 percent of their wealth to charities to address world poverty and other philanthropic initiatives. Since then, several other billionaires have followed their lead with similar pledges. On the surface, that seems like a lot of money being allocated to solve some critical world problems. One would think with that amount of money and that level of commitment to causes by these billionaires, there would be more proof of their success. However, the question becomes how big the problem is or whether these issues have to be addressed over more time—like the AIDS epidemic in Africa, which was addressed by President George W. Bush and Condoleezza Rice during the Bush presidency.

On the other side of the spectrum, a young man of twelve years old, Jaxson Turner, one of my protégés, simply wakes up in the mornings during the summer months and prepares his lemonade, salads, and other snacks. He then has his mother drive him to Elite Kutz barber shop. Finally, Jaxson sets up his stand and sells his products to random strangers on the street. He sells his products to raise money for his nonprofit organization to buy school supplies for children at his school who otherwise might not be able to afford them. I have more to say about this young man in chapter 16.

In fact, even if you have not been guided by your parents in a way that motivates you to speak English well, you must take charge of this very important accountability. Even if you have never been outside the borders of the country, you should be that person walking around speaking the Queen's English—accent and all. I am not in any way saying you shouldn't retain your slang, your jargon, your broken English, your colloquial, your dialect, or any of that. What I am saying is that when the time comes, and in cases where it is appropriate, you should speak English, and you should speak it well. In an important interview, you should speak English. In class, when you're asking questions or answering them, speak English. If you are presenting to an executive at your company, speak English. When you are speaking to your children, speak English so that they will . . . speak English!

Pursuing your happiness may take you to other countries. So you must be prepared. Children of the United States—I implore you to be accountable for learning a second language. Furthermore, I suggest you start first by learning Spanish. Even if other children are unwilling, I am saying directly and specifically to Black American children: you would be remiss not to follow through on this very important accountability. I, like most Americans, have lived my entire life not knowing a second language well enough to communicate with a person from a different country. I am incapable of speaking (fluently) a second language. It is one of my most regretful impediments. US citizens are perceived as arrogant in this regard. Now I am committed to learning at least one other language.

Once when I was in Cancun, Mexico, I witnessed three young US college students yelling at one of the Mexican servers. They were saying repeatedly, "Speak English, m*****f****." It was disgraceful to witness arrogant US citizens attempting to force a Mexican in his own country to speak English because they had not taken the time to learn any Spanish. I decided to put my book aside on the lounge chair and walk over to the young men from the US. I spoke very clear English combined with some of my colloquialisms and a few other choice words as I spoke to the shameful trio. Before I could finish providing my constructive feedback, the young men left with perplexed looks on their faces. They must have thought I was crazy.

I suggest all children and teenagers pursue happiness with dignity, class, and respect—especially respect for the differences of people in our country. Enjoy your life while commanding respect from others. God knows you will have earned it.

14

Integrity Life Principle: Respect

One would think respect is a relatively easy, intangible thing to manage. It is not. Respect is hard to manage because you have control over only one half of it. The other half is controlled and dictated by other people—including people you don't know. Respect has to do with the way your character, values, opinions, behaviors, style, and gestures are viewed and measured by others.

In the United States, most ordinary citizens dedicate their lives to earning and retaining respect. A person's level of success often hinges on the perceived level of respect the person has in varying settings or aspects of their lives, such as at home, at work, in public, at church, etc. Our citizenry pursues and places respect on a pedestal even when the definition of respect suggests perfection.

Merriam-Webster's defines respect as follows:

"High or special regard. The quality or state of being esteemed."

In terms of the two WIN life principles, respect is weighed more heavily. In fact, even if you are totally accountable and make really smart choices over the course of your life, if you present yourself in ways deemed inappropriate or vulgar, your good deeds could be disregarded. Respect is important because it serves the purpose of opening new doors of opportunity and gaining access to the kinds of relationships that could blossom into varying levels of value. On the other hand, respect is as simple as one person appreciating another's personal views or values. By the way, it is possible to disagree with a person's position on a particular topic while at the same time respecting their position.

Disrespect, on the other hand, especially constant premature disrespect of a certain people in a culture, establishes a norm that other citizens seem to easily conform to. Black Americans have been victims of the kinds of treatment, prejudgment, and stereotypes that cause ordinary citizens and sometimes people visiting here to paint negative views of Black Americans with a broad brush. The most innocent of Black Americans are impacted by this phenomenon. Nonetheless, the issue of disrespect for us is real and twofold.

The first concern is supported by a societal norm that has been perpetuated for decades by factions of white Americans. The second is a self-inflicted dilemma that has been perpetuated by Black American people. While the respect life principle is not intended to be limited to Black Americans, I'm compelled to point out special circumstances that make it challenging for our citizens to earn and sustain the respect they deserve. It is a fact that respect is not always measured equally across all races. The respect dilemma is soundly rooted in the divides our citizens insist on clinging to: notions of classes, firm beliefs in superiority, and, moreover, the color of one's skin and outward differences. This reality exists not because of a significant cultural change or anything like that. It's always been that way since before, during, and after slavery. Again, it's one of those chronic illnesses that has been passed down through generations. It's how a five-letter word initially intended as an identifier of a race of people has metamorphosed into a powerful connotation that explicitly labels everything associated with the word "black" bad. It seems the only use of the word "black" in positive terms is in terms of money or profit on a profit-and-loss statement.

The word "black" is inextricably attached to Blacks, Black Americans, and/or African Americans. Consequently, this faction of citizens is almost always prejudged negatively. Therefore, many Black Americans are constantly forced to prove themselves worthy of respect while other citizens enjoy the benefit of doubt. Far too often, with Black Americans, the prejudgments serve as roadblocks to success. This intentional social conflict has been profoundly pervasive and effective

Perspective

A simple doll study shows how the color black has been systemically linked to Black American people in a negative fashion. In the 1940s, husband and wife Dr. Kenneth Clark and Dr. Mamie Clark (both doctors in psychology) conducted a number of racial experiments to "measure the effects of segregation on Black American children." The experiments were widely acclaimed and became known as "the doll tests." They involved Black American children between the ages of three and seven and dolls that were mostly similar, except in color. In simple terms, the children were asked various questions related to which of the dolls they liked the best, which of the dolls they thought were bad or pretty, and so on. Consistently, the Black American children selected the white doll when asked about good or positive attributes (e.g., "Which doll is pretty?"). On the other hand, the Black American children consistently selected the black doll when asked to identify the doll with bad or negative attributes.

Fast forward from the 1940s. In 2010, Anderson Cooper conducted a modern-day version of the doll test. The outcomes were essentially the same as in the 1940s experiment. Cooper used images of dolls with declining shades of brown skin on a piece of paper, with one white doll image on the left end of the spectrum. Cooper asked a Black American boy, "What skin color do you want to be?" The boy pointed and eventually touched the whitest image of the doll on the paper. When Cooper asked the boy, "Why do you want that skin color?" the boy responded, "I don't know." Cooper then asked a girl, also Black American, "What color would you like to be?" The young Black American girl pointed and then touched the doll image to the right of the image that was the whitest on the paper. Cooper asked the girl, "Why did you choose that image?" The girl responded, as she pointed to the skin on her own face and arm, "Because it looks whiter than this kind." The girl pointed at the skin on her arm again and said, as she next pointed to the darker brown images on the paper, "This looks a lot like that." The girl then (without being prompted) said, "I don't like the way brown looks . . . because brown looks really nasty for some reason. But I don't know what reason."

In a different scene on the video, a different woman interviewed a white little girl. The woman asked the white girl, "Which of them is dumb?" The white girl—seemingly surprised by the question—responded, "Dumb?" as she expressed a short laugh; she responded by touching the darkest doll on the paper and said, "That one." When the lady asked the white girl why she chose that one, the white girl responded unequivocally, "Because she's Black."

This simple experiment represents a microcosm of the kinds of problems and confusion Black American children face and will continue to face because of the perpetuation of racism and discrimination in the United States. While all children of all races must earn respect, Black American children have an extra hurdle to clear. But to be clear, all shades of black skin are beautiful. Furthermore, every Black American child in the entire word clings to an unmistakable beauty reserved especially for them. There is no need for even a single Black American child to apologize or feel bad about their dark skin—embrace it, for God has given you the skin that is often the envy of others. Wear your skin, my child—wear it with the grace of a princess or a prince. Wear it in the daylight, noon, and at night. Wear it proudly as your strength and with your head held high. But in the end, know that because of your skin, you have a little extra work to do. So do it—do it for the sake of moving on to prominence and prosperity. As the great orator Martin Luther King once said, "Don't let anybody take your manhood." And don't let anyone take your womanhood either. Respect yourself first! It's the best way to validate and appreciate the importance of respecting others.

But some of the issues related to respect among Black Americans and in Black American communities are clearly self-inflicted. I'm that guy—the guy who decided way back in the early 1980s not to use the n-word ever again. I cannot change the will of others to stop using it; however, I can leverage my authority within my space—my home, for instance.

I made my views regarding the use of the n-word in my house to my close friends several years ago. It was a simple rule: I did not want anyone using it in my home. It turned out to be a somewhat bumpy process getting all my friends to conform. However, they do to this day. I didn't realize how many of them used the n-word. In fact, I was a little shocked that many of my friends, who are professionals—some of them executives in major Fortune companies—use it.

One day when I was hosting a viewing of an NFL game—the Washington Redskins versus the New York Giants—I was standing in my kitchen, entertaining a few of my guests while at the same time stealing glances at the last two minutes of the game through my peripheral vision. Just as the game was about to end and the outcome would be determined by the result of a field goal, the play started. The kicker of the Washington Redskins made the field goal, and the Redskins were just seconds away from winning the game. Needless to say, there was some intense emotion and commotion in my house. When it was official that the Redskins had won the game, my friend David Crow released his extraordinary excitement. He started yelling and jumping up and down and loudly referred to the opposing team—my team—as n-words. He said, "We kicked those n-words . . ."

I was still standing in the kitchen when I heard Crow's outburst from the opposite side of the countertop that separates the kitchen from the family room, where the main television is mounted on the wall. As I looked at Crow, I noticed him looking back at me with a slight smirk on his face. I could tell he knew I was disappointed. Within a few seconds, he walked around the counter and came directly to me, interrupting the conversation I was having with another friend. He asked me if we could talk. I agreed. Then he asked me to walk with him to the foyer area in my home. I did.

He looked me straight in my eyes and said, "Man—I apologize." I didn't immediately respond, and he went on to tell me how he had gotten caught up in the moment and that he did not mean to be disrespectful. He apologized again, and I accepted his apology.

"Crow . . ." I began but paused for several seconds. "Don't use that word in my home again."

"I hear you, man," he said, "and I'm really sorry." We shook hands, pulled each other close, traded the traditional Black American pat on the shoulder, and that was it. It has never happened again.

Crow has a body like Lou Ferrigno. Maybe I'm giving him too much credit, but in that moment at my home, my friend who is huge and trains seven days a week humbled himself to offer me respect. That's what real friends do. We respect each other unconditionally, and that means respecting each other's values.

On the other hand, not all of my friends were willing to conform to my simple request regarding the use of the n-word in my house. One friend, after he used it in my home and I (again) asked him not to do it again, replied, "N-word, please!" He and a few others got a good laugh from the experience. For me, it was one of those things where if I were twenty years younger, there would have been a fight. However, those days are gone, and I'm so much bigger than that now, maturity speaking. So, I simply lost respect for that person. And while I tolerate him, our friendship is not and will never be the same.

Imagine if all the citizens of the United States simply respected one another. Imagine if every Black American respected every other Black American. Our entire country would be a better place, our race would be noticeably different, and the 2060s project would likely just fall into place.

Parents

I suggest unequivocally that any parent who teaches or allows their children (regardless of race) to use the n-word going forward is teaching their child to disrespect themselves. I do not appreciate Jay-Z and other rappers using the n-word in their work. I respect that they have monetized it. But I can only hope and pray they will use some of their fortunes to support the next generation of children on their quest to the 2060s. I am hopeful the use of the n-word will be totally eradicated.

I disagreed with Ice Cube when he went on the Bill Maher show to proclaim (referring to the n-word), "That's our word now." Well, it may be his word. Furthermore, it may be the word of other rappers and ordinary Black Americans. That's their choice. However, it's not my word, and it is not the word of our children, who are making conscious choices to move on from that place of darkness to bigger, better, smarter, and more meaningful things.

Parents must teach their children about the kinds of behaviors that could serve as self-inflicted disrespect. Respect is about your character and how you choose to present yourself in the public's eye. Your comportment could make the difference in terms of whether you will be respected or disrespected, live or die, succeed or fail. It's time for parents and adults to step up their game in the respect arena. In this regard, our children need answers today and early in their lives.

If you know your child is a bully, you should have a conversation with them to make clear that bullying someone is more a sign of weakness than it is a sign of strength. The bully lacks courage and respect; thus, they seek it via a process of attempting to make others in their realm appear weaker. Who wants to be that person? You should be teaching your child to command respect with poise. Teach them how to command respect when they walk in a room because people will know their values. They will know because they will have witnessed your child helping others. They will know because your child will be the one opening the doors for the elderly. They will know because your child will be the one who doesn't mind playing but will often be found reading a book. People will remember your child as the one with the highest grade point average whom other students seek out for help.

Boys must be taught to respect girls early in their lives. When I was told by my son Cody's third grade teacher that he had inadvertently pushed a girl to the ground and had not helped her up, I taught him a lesson about respecting girls over an entire weekend. After spanking Cody for imposing his trickery on me by faking an asthma attack and having me pick him up from school early, I had made a conscious decision not to spank him again. So instead, I made him join what I called my girls boot camp. Cody's punishment was that he had to clean the entire two-story house inside and outside for the entire weekend. He was guaranteed three meals per day. He was also allowed three required breaks. During his breaks, he was required to sit with me and listen to my lectures (sometimes for over an hour) about why he should never hit or push or disrespect girls. I believe sitting through the speeches was harsher than having to vacuum, clean the baseboards, mop the floors, mow the lawn, clean the windows, wash the dishes, do the laundry . . . you get the point.

I can tell you right now that if you willfully use the n-word in front of your child, your child will start using it and may use it for the rest of their life.

Tell your son when he smells bad, and then make him take a shower. Don't let your child get to a place of complacency regarding his hygiene. Don't give him a chance to tolerate his own odor.

Inspire your child to be best in class. Smart kids are the ones who command respect, from the principal to the bully.

Be sure to help your child appreciate the value of dressing nicely and occasionally wearing a tie.

The one thing you will not need to teach your child when they are absolutely best in class is the way they dress, look, and smell.

Just be sure to teach them to be best in class at something!

Children

Make no mistake about this: people are watching your every move. Moreover, they are judging you, the way you stand, the way you speak, your clothes, your style, your shoes, the way you eat, and even your toes and feet. They will judge the way you smell. Every single thing you do will be judged. Therefore, if you choose to walk around with your pants hanging off your butt, people will look at you and treat you like you're walking around with your pants hanging off your butt—or with less than the respect you may think you deserve. It's natural for people to observe you and establish an opinion about the values you hold. With accountability, your choices are held within your mind until you make a choice to physically do something or take an outward action that is exposed to the public.

I know people who spend hours at the mall people watching and making internal judgments about random strangers. But you also get to communicate your values to people within your circle. Let people know what you like and don't like. This gives them a fair chance to respect your values.

But respect is not limited to people. Children must respect the realities of their circumstances. For instance, while it may be OK for other children to play with toy guns, that is not the case for young Black American children. If you refuse to acknowledge this potential danger, you could be legally shot to death for simply playing with a toy gun.

One of the best ways to command respect is to be smart and well read. People are always intrigued by readers. At some point in your life, you will be asked about what genre of books you read most. If you are unable to answer the question and list the latest books you have read, your respect will diminsh in the eyes of the person asking the question. Reading skills and higher education will develop your views on a broad range of topics. In addition, being smart commands respect in the job search process and when you reach that age when you're open to dating. Some girls like guys who are not so smart—but not for long. Conversely, some boys like girls who are not so smart—but for too long.

Different levels of respect exist based on your life goals. If you decide to develop yourself for a professional job in the workforce, then you must present yourself in ways that command respect. If you think major corporations are not willing to check out your posts on Facebook, Instagram, and Twitter to get an idea of who you really are and your values, you are sadly mistaken. They will! In that process, if they determine you have limited respect for yourself and others, you will be consequently overlooked.

I was in the barber shop recently when two young men were approaching the entrance straight ahead. However, as they got closer to the barbershop entrance, a young woman with two young girls approached from the left. The two men opened the door, and one by one they walked in the entrance of the barbershop, completely ignoring the woman and her daughters. It was unacceptable behavior. Men should be seeking opportunities to respect women. Had I witnessed the two young men in question open the door for the woman and her daughters, my friends will tell you that I would have been the first to walk over to them, shake their hands, and commend them for their respect of women.

Regarding your integrity, the respect life principle is so critically important. For that reason, I have a whole laundry list of tips that I believe all children should consider and take very seriously.

Tips
- Wear your faith on your sleeve.
- Read regularly while continuously improving your vocabulary—you will command respect each time you speak.
- Take your homework seriously. Command respect by being best in class.
- Learn a second language. You will be respected on the international stage. Ebonics is not a second language.

- Black American children and children around the world, *stop* using the n-word. Leave it in the 2010s. You and only you hold the power to eradicate this disgraceful word from all languages by the end of the 2060s.
- Girls—don't fall for disrespectful young men. Men should honor you, and you should always demand respect. Don't settle.
- Young men—don't *ever* hit a girl or a young woman. Such an act represents an extraordinary sign of weakness. Respect and protect girls and young women. As my mother would say, "You know better."
- Always show respect for other people, especially your elders.
- Tell the truth even when it makes others uncomfortable.
- Don't ever take anything that is not yours.
- Don't be "that guy" or "that girl"—the bully.
- Listen to your parents. However, be mindful that some of what parents teach is not always aligned with popular views and what is right. In this regard, know that as you continue to mature, you will be the one responsible for establishing your own values and your own character. You will become the judge.
- Don't conform to the teaching of principles that you fundamentally believe to be counter to your personal values.
- Respect the rule of law. You *do not* want to get caught up in the US penal system.
- "Trash talkin," slang, colloquialisms, and idioms have their place; however, you should master the English language and be prepared to use it over less informal habits of speech.
- You should always be mindful of the setting or environment you're in. The way you behave in the privacy of your home may not be appropriate in certain public settings.
- Learn proper dining etiquette, such as in terms of which fork to use when eating your entree versus the one to use for your salad or dessert.
- Be mindful of the way you dress because the way you dress says a lot about your character and your respect for others.
- Take good care of your hygiene. Young men—women don't like you when you smell bad. They just don't!

- You should always have at least one suit and a tie available for special occasions.
- If you have never felt the joy of knowing you actually helped someone who really needed your help, it is impossible for you to know the power of giving. Help somebody.

This short list is intended to lay a foundation for a child's respect barometer as we forge ahead to the 2060s. However, the actual list is infinite, so I can't cover everything. Nonetheless, I hope the stage has been set for young people to gain a clear understanding regarding what respect is and its importance. I hope this chapter will serve the purpose of shaping your integrity and your values. I learned the hard way that knowing right from wrong is not as binary as it seems. There is no cookie-cutter approach to this. However, the establishment of a sound set of base values will certainly serve a meaningful purpose. I challenge every child in the United States to regularly gauge their respect and integrity.

15

The Next Generation

Most parents have good intentions, and many of them do right by their children in terms of guiding them, preparing them for the workforce, and contributing to the shaping of their integrity. On the other hand, a larger faction of parents unintentionally fall way short of the same accountabilities. If most parents had gotten their accountability to nurture and appropriately groom and coach their children, there would be no need for me to write this book, and all would be good in the neighborhood. But that is unfortunately not the case.

It was necessary for me to put slavery in perspective in the early chapters of this book. However, this entire book is about the future of US children of all races—the next generation. Furthermore, this book is more about the future of this great nation, the United States of America. This book is about abandoning a dark past and forging new and amazing paths toward the future, ideally with significant milestones achieved by the end of the 2060s.

By engaging in the appropriate level of support of our children, the adults in their lives will ultimately dictate the social, political, economic, environmental, and race-related concerns of the future. It is important for all parents to first understand the extraordinary power of parenting and that their children, for the most part, turn out to be what they teach them to be.

Some parents taught their children how to be millionaires like them. Other parents taught their children how to be millionaires because they were not able to do it themselves. Countless parents taught their children the importance of maintaining and continuing the family structure. Many of them insisted their children get married and have children. However, not all parents were so keenly focused on the structure of the family. Some parents taught their children to love all people and to treat people with respect, while some taught their children to hate Black American people. Some parents taught their children to hate white American people. Others taught their children the value of appreciating and embracing the differences of people of all races. Others went the extra mile to instill cultural norms of superiority in their children. Some parents shaped their children with values that align with the nation's values; other nations', not so much. So, here we are.

Over the course of my career, several executives to whom I reported were compelled to remind me, "It is what it is." It was more than a suggestion that what I wanted to change just wasn't going to happen. I grew to hate the phrase. We are at a place right now where we can sit back with debilitating complacency and quietly say or believe our current situation "is what it is," or we can start today with smart, small steps to ensure things will change in the future. I am writing this book because I'm hopeful, and I believe in the will of the citizens of the United States to change, in spite of the current climate.

With that thought in mind, I'd like to introduce three focus areas for the next generation of children that should be guided by the adults in the room—parents and other adults willing to step up, make money, build relationships, and prosper.

Make Money

The United States may be conflicted in many ways in terms of certain social, economic, and racial concerns. However, there is one US cultural norm that 100 percent of citizens can agree upon—making money in this country is critically important and should be a peak priority. This is why the first three REWARDS life principles in the WIN Model are so important. As a recap, each child must be prepared to work in a job, own a business, or be an independent contractor. These are the three primary ways to make legitimate money.

The child's purpose for earning money will be firstly to appreciate the value of making money and secondly to survive on their own without the support of their parents or others. The long-term goal of making money will be to get to a place of building wealth.

Relationships

I read and heard from my friends a story regarding some of Russell Wilson's friends and teammates spreading rumors that Wilson was not "Black enough." Wilson's friends were referring to his choices of other friends and maybe the way he speaks. I am from Birmingham, Alabama, and I have no idea what it means to be "Black enough." Feel free to pull my Black card. To me, that perspective seems to be one of those self-inflicting headwinds that potentially impede Black American progress. It's like the parent who forces her child to apologize for speaking English by suggesting the child is sounding white. Having diverse friends and speaking English are both required in order to be successful. My honest view on this is that both suggestions are unequivocally nonsensical. Black Americans must be fully willing and prepared to do what it takes to WIN in the US. There will be no room for picking and choosing or dithering in the process of making moves. We have to be ready. Furthermore, I suggest that those of us who don't have at least three white fiends going forward toward the 2060s will not be "Black enough." Our goal is to break down these simple divides that make it harder than it should be to WIN in the country our ancestors built and funded with their free labor. In the end, when it all works out and the broad implementation of the WIN Model's seven REWARDS life principles start to prove successful, white Americans will be knocking on the doors of Black Americans just to be within our realm. That's how relationships work. That's what being best in class commands.

Beyond all that, our children's relationships will ultimately serve the purpose of further improving race relations. The question will then be, "Is it possible to completely eradicate racism in the United States over the next fifty years?"

Prosper/Wealth

Whenever our children work and get paid, they should be conditioned to save a portion of what they make. Having money and being smart about leveraging it will be of significant value later in life. While it has not been the case in the past, helping the next generation should always be a top priority. It should be part of a cyclical or recurring strategy. This approach will contribute to a plan with a mission declaring, "Never again." This is the best example of how wealth should be leveraged. This is the real way by which no child should be left behind.

I acknowledge my tone has been firm related to moving on, and I do not intend to offend anyone. Parents have the right to raise their children in the ways they see fit. However, I beg of you to ask yourself the following:

- Do you want your child to reach the 2060s using the n-word, illiterate, uneducated, unwilling to speak English, unemployed, and with their pants hanging halfway off their butt?
- Do you want your child to reach the 2060s limited in terms of their relationships and access to resources? Do you really want your black child to reach the 2060s in the absolute most diverse country in the world with just Black American friends, or your white child with just white American friends?
- Do you want your child to reach the 2060s broke and unable to support their family and the next generation of children, including their own?
- Do you want your child to reach the 2060s with firm and unshakable beliefs in superiority and racism? Do you want your child to cling to a notion that they're better for no reason other than that their skin is a certain color?

Think about it. This is exactly what's been happening since slavery ended more than 150 years ago. It's time to change. So, I am curious about the answers to these questions because these are the exact paradigms the majority of us seek to break. And the only way to break them is through our children.

Have you ever had a moment when you've reflected on your life and wondered how your outcomes would have changed had you been better informed? When you think about it, do you believe you would be a different person and in a better place or financial position had you been given the answers early in your life? Do you believe you would have managed certain situations differently? Do you think about whether or not certain information would have led you to make smarter life and career choices? If your answer to any of those questions was yes, you are not alone. I know that had I been guided appropriately—way back when I was five years old—my life and my lifestyle would be very different and so much better today. I know that had my parents and I not been impacted by racism, we would have had a better start.

Had there been a clear and concise plan laid out before me, I know, with a very high degree of certainty, I'd be in a completely different place right now. I would have reimagined my entire path with more care and focus on winning and succeeding. I would have achieved more, and I'd be capable of helping more people—more children. There is a very good chance I would have written this book more than twenty years ago, and today I'd be relishing in the success of that book, which may have been dubbed *The 2010s Project*. I'd be here measuring the success of the book in terms of the number of children positively impacted by the seven REWARDS life principles. I imagine there are millions of adults in the United States who share my sentiments—had they only known. Had they been guided the right way, their lives would be enhanced because they would have been taught to properly manage their lives and choose the right geographies to live in. However, like me, far too many of us simply lived our lives without the ideal structure—leaving our futures to chance. We settled by walking into doors that were just slightly open, with easy access, versus opening the closed ones and making new discoveries. Like so many others, I missed it in spite of the direction I received—a direction consequently limited in scope due to norms of superiority in the southeastern quadrant of the United States, where I was born and lived my childhood. Yes, many of us missed it, including some who were in other US geographies where the social headwinds of racism and superiority were not as prevalent and negatively impactful. Many missed the opportunity to dictate their own destinies because they simply failed to plan—and by default planned to fail. But it doesn't have to be that way going forward. Now is the time to start the process of breaking the vicious cycle of capitulation. Now, with the opportunity right in front of us, we must stand up to mitigate any chance of US children falling into the same trap. We must ensure our children are positioned and prepared with meaningful and constructive plans for their futures—plans complete with purpose.

There is a void in the US general family structure. Too many parents have deficits in terms of being forward thinkers and planners for their children and coaches for their teenagers. The idea of at minimum guiding your child to be great seems like less of a priority than giving them the greenlight to play games and buy the latest Jordans and Nike sneakers. Our culture seems retroactive to the future. Too consumed with present accommodations, opportunities to equip our children with the right values are repeatedly overlooked or, worse, never considered. We fall short of preparing our children for what's next. All of us could do a better job supporting our children. Even children could do a better job supporting other children. However, to do better, one must appreciate the values linked to giving and supporting others—especially those who we can easily determine are in need.

My mother, Catherine Harper, taught my siblings and me painful lessons about giving. In this regard, her love was insurmountable. Even with ten children of her own to feed, she made room at our small table and seats on the floor for the few of our neighbors who just happened to show up around dinner time on Sundays—the one day of the week when we had our best meal: fried chicken or smothered pork chops. The lessons were painful because I recall not having enough to eat, but I just didn't want a neighbor eating the food my mother worked so hard to provide for her children.

One day, at the appropriate time and with distance between my mother and me, I pulled one of my friends to the side and told him to go home to eat. He responded by telling me they didn't have food at their home like "Mrs. Hoppa's." I knew how good my mother's cooking was, so it didn't take long for me to understand. Then he told me there was no food at his house. I was shocked and decided to back off.

We did not have a lot, but there was always food at our house. Because of our living conditions—twelve family members staying in a small, three-room house—I thought we were poor. But not so much. To this day, my Aunt Elma will not allow any of us to even remotely suggest we were poor. My mother was the epitome of a provider. I have often said she passed away at the young age of sixty-two because she neglected her own health to give to her children. But this level of selflessness is not advised for the sake of this book's message; please do not neglect your health.

If you haven't felt the powerful sensation in your heart of knowing you did something to help someone else, you have been missing out on a profound pleasure of life. I know the feeling. I know because there is only one way to experience it. You must give to someone—unconditionally.

Several years ago, my friend Saundra called me about a mission trip her daughter Maddison was taking to certain villages in South Africa. She asked if I would mind if Maddison called to ask for support for her cause. I agreed and was eager to help. A day later, I received a very well-written email from Maddison in which she delineated her mission. She wanted me to provide T-shirts to be shipped to South Africa. When I asked how many T-shirts she needed, Maddison told me she needed as many as I could provide. My initial thought was that the shirts would be used for a softball team or something. After Maddison clarified that her goal was to send hundreds of shirts to multiple villages, I was perplexed. Maddison told me the shirts would be delivered to young girls to use as dresses. I finally understood, and I had the shirts shipped within a few days and never thought much else about the shipment. Several weeks later, I received pictures of young girls wearing the shirts I had shipped. They had silly phrases on them, like HABU with the subtitle "hook a brotha up." Another read, "Y'all Play Too Much." But as I watched the images of the African children wearing the silly shirts I sent them, I saw through the phrases and into the hearts of children pleased to have sufficient clothing—girls wearing T-shirts as dresses. It was then that I felt my blessing. Being in a position to help someone in need is something every human being should strive to experience.

You may never know if the panhandler on the street really needs food or not, but if they look the part, you'd be remiss not to help. Whether the panhandler imposes trickery on you and uses the money to buy alcohol or whether they use it to buy much-needed food, either way, you will be blessed for offering to help someone.

There is a very large faction of US citizens who are yearning for help—some of whom have no idea the kind or level of help they need. I'm talking about a very large pool of young children, children of all races and backgrounds—children of parents who simply do not know how to prepare their children for success. It is for this reason that children must start to bear the brunt of this responsibility. There is a huge challenge ahead of us. Children must help other children.

Chinese philosopher Lao Tzu once said, "Give a man a fish and you feed him for a day. Teach him how to fish and you feed him for a lifetime." Let's start today, feeding our children for life by imparting priceless knowledge to them. This book is intended to give them the answers.

The next generation is the final module of the WIN Model. This module included the final two REWARDS life principles:

• Duty or doing for others.
• Saving money and being financially astute.

Proof of how we got here from a very dark past is profoundly evident. The question is how much of the divisiveness we experience today is part of a structural plan. Children, through no fault of their own, were groomed and delivered the divisive norms we cling to by passing them down. So why not turn the tables by starting today, passing down a different set of values through our children—positive values fundamentally necessary for their success.

16

Next Generation Life Principle: Duty

While this has not always been the case, going forward, children have an accountability to contribute to the support of the next generation. I have witnessed children play very key and critical roles helping other children, and I have come to realize the power of such a dynamic. Sometimes the messages delivered to children by other children can be more compelling and meaningful than the same messages delivered by a biological parent or an adult. However, it is done; it must be done. Children must be taught the lessons of giving and supporting others.

The core intrinsic value of helping others is best taught via observation. For children to more clearly understand why certain people and children need help, they must witness the hardship firsthand, especially children from affluent families. Young children and teenagers must somehow be engendered to appreciate what it's like to live a substandard lifestyle like the ones lived by a very large groups of US citizens today. Our children must be led to the places in our country where homelessness and poverty are prevalent. They must at minimum witness poverty, as this experience can be humbling and contribute to the shaping of a person's core values. Children who read should imagine and anticipate the failures of the children who should be reading but are unable or struggling to do so. It's the kind of reality that touches the soul and inspires action.

Charity and the idea of duty or giving are not the kind of attributes that should be forced on a child. Children must be exposed to the dark and grim social and financial realities of other people in order to understand the needs of others and to garner the will to sustain a firm commitment to do something about it.

Consumers of music listen to the beats, dance along, and bounce their heads up and down in the process of enjoying the experience. However, far too often, they miss the powerful messages embedded in the lyrics—for instance, the message signaled by George Benson about the importance of children dictating the outcomes of our future and the powerful messages unmasked by Phil Collins regarding homelessness and the unwavering will of ordinary people to ignore the problem day in and day out in his song "Another Day in Paradise."

Collins features a homeless woman who I imagine, in her raspy voice, calling out to a male passerby to ask for help. The woman describes the cold air outside and indicates she doesn't have anywhere to sleep. She simply asks if the man would consider helping her. Collins continues with a description of the man's response as he glides away, never missing a step and pretending not to hear the homeless woman. Whistling as he walks across the street, the man is described as embarrassed to be in the predicament of ignoring the woman's needs and his unwillingness to help her. Then Collins reminds us all to at least think about giving or helping people in need.

The US Department of Housing and Urban Development issued a report that suggests there are approximately 65,000 homeless people in New York City and approximately 50,000 homeless people in Los Angeles. They live in cars, under bridges, in the subway tunnels, and on the sidewalks in almost every major and midsize city. The department estimated there are just under 554,000 homeless people in the United States, of which 15 percent are considered "chronically homeless"—a person with a disability who has been homeless for more than a year. Overall, 40.6 million people live below the poverty line in the United States. It is estimated that 13.3 million children under the age of 18 live below the poverty line in this country, the most prosperous nation in the world. Finally, it's worth stating again that 14 percent or approximately 32 million adults in the United States are considered illiterate.

There is no shortage of needs in the world. In fact, most US citizens will find a person or persons in need of help within a few miles of where they live.

Since it's not easy to reshape the lifestyles or situations of adults, we must keep asking this: What can we do to help? Those men who have rarely read books over the course of their lives will more than likely not start reading today or for the rest of their lives. The uneducated rarely have a change of heart and decide to go back to school. The people who choose to live in climates where economies are not conducive for measurable and sustained success are more likely to stay rather than make the decision to move to other thriving cities in the contiguous states. The homeless seem hopeless and unwilling to change their situations, or in most cases incapable of doing so. Despite the challenges our country faces and the sporadic gestures or interest in dealing with these kinds of calamities, people must continue making constructive efforts to improve and sustain the lives of our citizens impacted by hardship and inequality—if for no other reason than it's the right thing to do.

I completely understand the plight associated with grown men and women experiencing disparity. People in our country are dealing with drug addictions, alcoholism, and homelessness. We can never forget the elderly, the sick, and the physically and mentally challenged. It would be a mistake to ignore the poverty-stricken men and women in our country. However, I suggest the most critical person in need is the illiterate, uneducated, unemployed, unaccountable, disrespectful, broke child—the child whose plight has not yet been realized, who is still protected by the umbrella of parental care.

The only way to eradicate mounting disparities born of illiteracy, lack of education, and poverty in the United States is to pay forward by investing in our children today and very early in their lives. Then we'll be positioned to anticipate the intrinsic reward and count on our protégé's brightened futures—the same outcomes ordinary people will have contributed to.

Each time I think about the simplicity of how children grow up to be adults, I struggle to understand why parents don't do a better job of grooming their children for success and the future. We all know that children become educated, work most of their lives, get married, have children, and become business owners, politicians, and even presidents of the United States; so why don't we guide them better? Conversely, some parents choose to ignore the accountability of grooming their children. Nonetheless, the problem is not limited to ignorance. The problem, as with other norms, is passed down from decades ago when children's fates were unintentionally left to chance. Consequently, the roll-the-dice approach is more common than reliable approaches to generate positive futures for children.

Perspective

It was one of those hot, early Saturday mornings in Plano, Texas, in late June 2018. In anticipation of the daily silly bantering that's common at Elite Kutz, I was eager to get there to join in. However, I knew my schedule would not permit me to hang around long after my cut, as I needed to get back to my writing.

While I was sitting in the barber chair with the trademarked Elite Kutz cover tied around my neck and draped across my chest, my barber, Roy, in between his jokes, was carefully executing his skills of cutting and grooming the little hair on my head. In the fray of it all, I noticed a young boy outside with his mother getting out of the car. They started unfolding a table, and neatly spread a colorful plastic cloth over it. I asked Roy what the kid was doing. Roy literally stopped grooming my head, turned me around in the barber chair, looked me square in my eyes, and said, "That's a smart kid right there." Roy continued, "He sells lemonade during the summer months to make extra money." From what I had learned from Roy, the young boy and his character seemed indicative of the kind of hope I'd like to see more of. These are the young boys who take their futures seriously and mitigate the pitfalls that swallow our youth's chances of fulfilling lives.

It didn't take long before I was impressed. As Roy completed his mastery on my edges, the very short window required to finish grooming my bald head was about to expire. Between all the jokes, laughs, and craziness that happen every Saturday morning at Elite Kutz, we kept the conversation going—covering the need for more children to follow the young man's lead. When Roy had finished, in typical fashion, I paid him, made sure he had not stolen my Ray-Bans, laughed about that, gave him some dap, said my goodbyes, and wished everybody in the shop a great weekend. Then I headed to the door with full intentions of meeting the young man I had become so intrigued with.

After exiting the Elite Kutz and stepping into the blistering Texas heat, I encountered him. He was smaller than I had originally thought, but like a true businessman, his smile was infectious. He displayed the clear braces in his mouth, and I extended my hand to him. He returned the favor with a firm grip. I admire young men with firm handshakes. It's an indication of their confidence. I said to him, "So what's your name, young man?"

"Jaxson," he responded.

Then I asked, "What are you doing?"

He seemed eager to answer my question. However, after he started to answer me, his mother took a few steps in, interrupted Jaxson, and started telling me her version of what Jaxson was doing. Jaxson immediately interrupted his mother by looking up to her, stomping his right foot on the concrete pavement, and, with a slightly forceful but clearly respectful gesture, calling to his mother, "Mooom!" He paused, and his mother stopped talking. Jaxson continued, "Let me tell him." They both smiled at each other as his mother immediately and reluctantly surrendered to her son and stood there with that smile of pride on her face.

Jaxson continued with his story. He told me that he was selling lemonade so that he could use the money to buy school supplies for other children at his school who aren't able to afford them. I was dumbfounded. In fact, I was reduced to a simple response: "Wow!" I told Jaxson how proud I was of him for being so thoughtful and recognizing the needs of others less fortunate. Moreover, I told him how impressed I was that he was willing to go the extra mile to do something to help other children. Unfazed by my shock, Jaxson thanked me before he continued, "Yeah, it's sad to see children show up to school on the first day without school supplies. It makes me sad because I know it will be hard for them to keep up."

Jaxson continued to tell me that he had raised $12,500 so far, and his goal was $18,000. He was all about the business. He told me he would be in the same place selling lemonade for the rest of the summer until he reached his goal and invited me to come back to show my support by buying more of his products. Then Jaxson's mother started to chime in again, "Yeah, he's been recognized by the mayor of Dallas, Mayor Rawlings." She continued, "Oh, and President Obama gave him a shout-out once. He's been on the radio."

But as his mother rolled Jaxson's accomplishments off her tongue, he simply smiled as he continued to focus on his business, supporting his team of friends helping him sell lemonade. He was less interested in (and embarrassed by) all the accolades and more eager to raise the money and meet or exceed his goal.

But Jaxson came back to me, and we continued our talk for at least another fifteen minutes or so. I donated to his cause; however, I initially declined the cup of lemonade he offered me in return. He was pleased with my donation, so he again offered me the cup of lemonade. It was clear he did not want something for nothing. So, I accepted Jaxson's lemonade. He gave me a hug around my waist as he showed off that big smile with the clear and barely noticeable braces on his teeth. We took a picture together before he went back to work, selling lemonade and other healthy items, like salads his mother had whipped up a special dressing for.

I witnessed Jaxson swiping credit cards through the square plugged into the bottom of his phone. At the end of each transaction, he offered his customers a receipt from his nonprofit organization and asked if they wanted it emailed to them.

For several weeks in the summer of 2018, I went back to Elite Kutz, and there he was, selling lemonade to buy school supplies and backpacks for the sole purpose of making it easier for young children to keep up in school and receive a healthy education. You see, Jaxson knows that education is and should be every child's absolute number-one priority. Therefore, Catherine Harper for Keepers (CH4K.net), a nonprofit organization founded in my mother's name that aligns with and is connected to President Obama's My Brother's Keeper Alliance, provides donations and support of Jaxson's Never too Young to Care nonprofit (N2Y2C.org).

I know with a strong degree of confidence that there are young teens who have mastered most or all the seven REWARDS life principles—education being one of them. I also know that many of these same young teens are not fully aware of the value they could be adding by leveraging their parents' teachings and their good upbringings to do something especially smart to support other children who through no fault of their own experience disadvantages. We must teach our children the value of doing for others. Teenagers must be inspired—adults must inspire them to pay close attention and play active roles in the development of other children in ways that ensure the recycling of the right values in the minds of younger children. Although I met him only while writing this book, Jaxson is clearly one of my absolute best examples of the kind of young men it will take to solve our country's problems linked to inequality and disparity. However, I'd be remiss not to acknowledge that his values are embedded within his mind and spirit because of the strong will of his mother and her teachings.

Most of us aren't forward thinkers. But think about it. Jaxson will be more than sixty years old by the end of the 2060s. He's off to an amazing start. His possibilities are endless. His life outcomes will be monumental. Now, think about all the other thousands of young children who will follow his lead and those of other children like him.

Homelessness, illiteracy, lack of education, unemployment, unaccountability, disparity, racism, discrimination, and all headwinds associated with adult citizens impact our children.

Parents

Your children and teenagers don't always fully understand the power they possess to dictate their own lives and the lives of other children. Nor do children fully appreciate that they will eventually be the ones to make major and significant contributions to the society they live in. Often, parents are too preoccupied with teaching and forcing their children to just be children. A child's life is so much bigger than a childhood, and parents and other adults own the accountability to expose their children to the bigger picture of life.

For every poor child in this country, there are thousands of children far less fortunate around the world. Our children need to know this. Children born in the United States are among the most fortunate children in the entire world. Do not allow your child to take it for granted. Teach your child about the extraordinary opportunities they have to succeed here. Teach them about their ownership and accountability to shape their life outcomes. Be sure to teach your child about the importance of being prepared and developed for the workforce. Make sure your child's integrity is on point. More importantly, guide your child in ways that motivate them to eagerly help and drive other children to their fullest potential.

Tell your children the truth: despite how harsh it may be, they are citizens of the most prosperous nation in the world. Therefore, there is absolutely nothing powerful enough to prevent or minimize their goals and related potential to succeed—*nothing!*

Parents, please be mindful and honest that you're not perfect. We have all made mistakes—the kinds of painful mistakes that became too late to address. Don't let your child make the same ones you made. Please don't allow your children to live their lives by chance. Make sure your child is deliberate in their life choices and purposeful with their goals and missions. If your child does not understand the importance of voting and participating in the US election process, you will be complicit in their decision to stay home on election days when they are old enough to vote.

Unlike the gloomy days of the 150 years since slavery ended, our children now have the right, the climate, the opportunities, the hopeful signs, the examples, and everything else required to succeed. Once your child has benefited and been shaped by these modern amenities, teach them how to guide and support others who may be less fortunate, younger, or simply misguided. The adults are the ones who need to stand up for this quest to the 2060s by preparing their young soldiers to own the change.

While the heading of this section suggests parents should be the ones leading in the development of our children, teachers have a particularly important role as well. Mentors, guardians, and any adult willing and able to make meaningful contributions to children's lives should acknowledge this challenge for the future of our country and the good of humanity.

Children

Children helping and guiding other children in positive ways is the most powerful assertion in this entire commentary. Parents own the initial accountability of shaping their children's lives; however, children must be prepared to take the helm of their own life's journey early.

Children of the United States have a unique opportunity and duty to pay it forward with their time and resources in support of guiding other children. They will ultimately own the perpetuation of the kinds of values known to enhance the life outcomes of other children. Imagine for a moment the young teenager who makes a very conscious choice to mentor a ten-year-old child. The child may be the teen's brother, cousin, neighbor next door, or a child at an afterschool center for kids. The teen sets the best examples for the child by publicly displaying his passion for reading. The teen engenders the child to read regularly. The teen reads with the ten-year-old, forming routines. The teen achieves a firm commitment from the young girl that she will read a minimum of five pages per day. Initially, the child consistently falls short of her goal. Eventually, she starts to lead by proactively approaching her new mentor, eager to tell him about the new books she's reading. This is exactly what should be happening with young children across the entire United States. Imagine if the aforementioned scenario was happening with all seven of the REWARDS life principles— reading, education, work, accountability, respect, duty for others, and saving. By any means necessary, we must instill these seven life principles and other virtues within the minds of children, starting as early as three to five years old. That's the role teenagers should be playing right now.

Some teens are misinformed in terms of the value they could be adding by leveraging their parents' teachings and their good upbringings to do something especially smart to support other children who, through no fault of their own, may be at severe disadvantages. Teens, you should not remain idle, waiting on your parents to guide you in this regard. Feel free to step up as Jaxson did. Teens have a duty to teach others to play active roles in the development of other children. They must lead the way in the recycling process of more teens with the right values instilled in them.

Tips

- All young children should know each of the seven REWARDS life principles and live by them, starting early in their lives and for the rest of their lives.
- Children will be accountable for purposefully passing down the REWARDS life principles to other children and their own.
- Teach a child to teach another child; show them the value of this extraordinary level of giving so they will be eager to lead the way going forward.

- Children should be regularly reminded of their duty to support other children.
- Discuss with your child the importance of their knowing and appreciating the change they will be responsible for as they grow older and into adulthood.
- Allow your child to volunteer, and in some cases insist on it. Use the teachable experience to ensure your child learns a very clear lesson about the value of giving.
- Make sure your child uses some of their saved money to donate to a cause.
- Take your child to a homeless shelter.
- Take your child to events to feed the homeless on Thanksgiving and Christmas.
- Drive your child through poverty-stricken neighborhoods.
- Sponsor your child's missionary trip to a foreign country in Africa or just south of the border in Mexico.

The idea of supporting the next generation will be critical as we start this new journey to the 2060s. After one child is guided properly, ideally, they will be eager to do something for another. If for any reason, this critical cycle of supporting the next generation is broken, the entire national strategy to save our children and our country will fail.

I will cover the importance of there being a cohesive plan to instill the WIN Model's seven REWARDS life principles within the minds of children in chapter 18. It's important our children understand that the roles they play going forward will supersede the roles adults and parents will play. This is important because children often conform to and appreciate the views and styles of their older friends and idols. Younger children look up to older ones. Therefore, as long as the teenager is onboard with properly guiding his protégé in alignment with the WIN Model, the positive outcomes of such pairings could prove substantial. This level of mentoring could represent the best example of the kind of natural progression into the future—the 2060s. Children supporting other children—especially those who may be at a disadvantage—could become one of the cornerstones of the WIN Model.

17

Next Generation Life Principle: Saving Money

Saving money requires an extraordinary level of discipline—especially with children. Teaching children to save the money they earn will turn out to be a process. The key is to first make sure children understand the importance of saving money, but therein lies the problem.

As I have written this book, I've realized how serious people are about living in the now. It was easy to come to this realization because I'm writing a book about the future. Picture that! Anyway, getting your child to save for the future can be a daunting task with profound rewards attached. But once you clear the hurdle, it's all gravy from that point on. Unfortunately, most parents, like me, will get it wrong because they missed opportunities to save themselves.

The proper way to save money is to take a very structured and serial approach. I suggest there are four high-level steps in the saving-money process. They are:

1. Making money
2. Spending money on nondiscretionary goods and services
3. Spending money on discretionary goods and services
4. Saving money

Making Money

In order to make money legally, you must have a legitimate job or own some level of a legitimate business. I have covered extensively the best way to land a well-paying job in chapter 8 (on workforce development) and the three REWARDS life principles' chapters associated with workforce development in chapters 9, 10, and 11.

The level at which you are skilled will ultimately determine the amount of money you make. Your education level and the discipline or type of work you choose as a career will also play a role in determining how much you make. Ideally, you want to make as much money as you can. Just be sure your approach to making money is totally legal.

Spending Nondiscretionary Money

Nondiscretionary money is spent on goods and services that are required, and there is no flexibility. These goods and services must be secured or purchased because they are critical to your living, the sustainment of your life, and your freedom. Taxes are the number-one nondiscretionary expenditure. Other nondiscretionary items might include rent, mortgage, utilities (gas and electricity), food and water, and transportation.

Spending Discretionary Money

Discretionary money should be spent on goods and services that are not required for critical situational living and survival needs. These goods and services are usually related to your entertainment and social agenda. They include movies, music, extra clothes, expensive purses and shoes, jewelry, vacations, concerts, gifts, home improvements, etc.

Saving Money

The money you get to save is the money left over after you make money, spend the money you are required to spend (nondiscretionary), and spend the money you have flexibility to spend or not spend (discretionary).

Saving money is so important that Elizabeth Warren came up with a rule for saving. The rule suggests 50 percent of the money you earn should be spent on nondiscretionary goods and services, 30 percent should be spent on discretionary goods and services, and 20 percent should be saved. While this model may not work if you are making minimum wage, it should work if you are in the middle class earning in the upper five figures, $50,000 to

$90,000 a year. Furthermore, it may be possible to actually save more than 20 percent of your earned cash if you earn $100,000 or more. In the end, when you start making a lot of money, your lifestyle will play a key role in terms of the amount of money you can save.

Perspective

US citizens do not save money in the quantities they should. Several reports estimate that more than 50 percent of Americans have less than $1,000 in a savings account. As with most metrics used to measure and present economic statuses, Black Americans' financial situations fall behind whites—much like the unemployment rate for Black Americans, which for years has been consistently double the national average. This life principle, saving money, is all about changing that reality.

I am especially concerned about Black Americans, who since the end of slavery and since becoming full citizens of the United States have always had to deal with economic headwinds systemically imposed via laws and, more often, illegal practices designed to mitigate or slow their progress. It's the conversation no one wants to have. Nonetheless, Black Americans have an accountability to do all they can within their power to handle the side of the equation they have total control over. A large part of that includes instilling the seven REWARDS life principles in their children, including but not limited to the life principle of saving money.

I have made my mistakes in this regard. But here I am now, pleading with Black American children and children of all races not to make the same mistakes I made in my life when I was a child and to this point in my life. I am compelled to make a stand to get every child on the right track—starting with reading and ending with money.

In 1975, a singing group named the O'Jays released a song titled "Living for the Weekend." The lyrics explicitly outlined a plan to use the money made from working all week long to party all weekend. It was a common theme in my hometown of Birmingham, Alabama. Back in those days, the weekends represented a brief time window to be used almost solely for calming the disquiet of the stress of the work week and the inconveniences of racism and discrimination. In retrospect, the weekends also represented justification for not being smarter about managing money and planning forward. Most of us simply lived in the now, with little to no interest in the future—maybe because there was always a lingering question as to whether the future was even guaranteed, as hopelessness lingered over our heads like clouds. It was what it was—the way by which far too many of us carelessly lived our lives outside our financial means. We bought and consumed too much of nothing. Consequently, many of us rarely had much to show for our hard work. As for me, I was too busy trying to be super fly. I started working at Prince Hall Apartments when I was a freshman at Jackson-Olin High School. The extra money I made I spent on clothes and shoes—cheap clothes and shoes. My bell-bottoms covered my cheap gray boots. The waistbands on my pants were at least five or six inches high and almost reached my skinny, bony chest. I weighed about 150 pounds or less. The other pair of pants I wore with a high waistband were longer and completely covered my platform shoes with a rope-like material around the tall part of the soles. I almost broke my ankles—both—five times. On occasion, I wore suits to school, complete with a tie. I would even carry a briefcase. One day when it wasn't cold at all, I decided to wear a fake fur coat to a Jack-Olin High School football game. Some of the girls liked the swag. However, I knew I looked like a fool. To this day, when I visit my brother, Fred, at his house in Birmingham, Alabama, he always asks me if I remember that time I wore the fake fur coat to the game when it was ninety-five degrees. He thinks it's the funniest thing ever. He tells his boys the story all the time. It's one of those childhood things that only a brother will cling to and remind you of.

I guess I wanted to feel like I was somebody important. I wanted to be noticed and popular. I wanted to be somebody, somebody like the elderly neighbor in our community, Mr. Joe, had told me I'd be, even though I had no idea what he meant when he said, "You Catherine's boy, huh? One of dem Hoppa's, ain't cha."

I responded, "Yes, sur."

He'd continued, "Which one are you? There's so many of you I lose count." Then he laughed a little with his mouth closed—his lips clinched—so as not to spit out the tobacco he was chewing.

I responded, "Yes, sur, my name is Ralph."

Mr. Joe respond, "Boy, you sho lookin good, you gone be somebody, ain't cha?" Then he laughed again the same way he had before.

I responded, "Yes, sur," and then went on my way.

I didn't get the impression he was laughing at me or at his own joke. He was hopeful for me. I could tell because in those days, even when grown men and women were dealing with their own hopelessness, they remained hopeful for young girls and boys like me. They were hopeful that time would ultimately be the basis for change.

When I graduated from Jackson-Olin High School, the class of 1979, I was voted "Best Dressed." I'm not sure why, but I was also voted "Most Likely to Succeed." I was recognized again in our class yearbook for serving as president of the Future Business Leaders of America (FBLA). In the end, all the accolades meant absolutely nothing to me. They had no value because in the summer of 1979, the saddest reality consumed my thoughts as I was planning to attend Talladega College. Even though I still had my job at Prince Hall Apartments, I was broke. I was broke because I consciously made bad choices to misuse the money I made working over the course of four years while I was still in high school. I traded it all in for some big cheap bell-bottoms with tall waistbands, some gray boots with zippers on the side, a used cheap fur coat, and a lot of other dumb and wasteful stuff when I should have been saving my money for the future so that I could use it for something meaningful like college. This is just one of my "hindsight is twenty-twenty" moments. As I have said time and time again, the value of knowledge is zero unless you use the knowledge in a way that makes it valuable. Therefore, I am hopeful thousands of people will read this story and absorb the knowledge related to what they shouldn't do with their money. That way they will save it and make a world of difference in their lives and the lives of others within their realm. Please do not make the same mistakes I made as a young boy so many years ago. Be smart. Save your money, and use it wisely.

Parents

Your child must be eighteen years old to open a checking or savings account on their own. However, if your child is between fourteen and seventeen years old, they can open a bank account with your consent and with you as the cosigner on the account.

Teaching your child the value of saving should be at the top of your parenting accountability. Parents must be proactive about clearing the hurdles of making sure their children understand the value of saving by having a plan in place early in their child's life. When your child is too young to have a bank account, they can save money in a jar or a porcelain piggybank. However, as soon as your child is old enough to do so and is serious about saving money, you'll need to open their bank account. If you are not able to get your child excited about saving money, your child may struggle to manage money later in life.

Bank accounts are key because it is not as easy to spend money that is sitting in a savings or checking account at a bank.

I cannot stress enough the importance of saving. It is always relative to individual predicaments. For instance, if your parents are very wealthy, your concern about saving or your need to save might be a moot point. Otherwise, you will more than likely save your money for the distant future. I would hope the child from an affluent family would be eager to use more of their savings to help others (including teaching them about the idea of saving) who may be at a disadvantage. You should be eager to save for several reasons. After all, one of the main reasons anyone should save money is to ensure it will not be financially disruptive or painful when they pay forward to help another cause.

On the other hand, the child from a family with limited means will have different priorities, which might be dictated by unique circumstances. The child from a family with limited means might make their education their number-one priority so as not to put that burden on their parents' shoulders and to be better positioned (financially) to help others in the future. Otherwise, the child with limited means may find it necessary to use their savings to help cover the cost of living in their family. That's how things turn out sometimes.

Children

To save money and be financially astute, you must earn money. As I have stated several times, when you are old enough to work, you should be working. This means that if your parents are willing to pay you an allowance for doing chores at your home (even if you are just eight years old), it's time to go to work, start saving some of your money, and become financially responsible. I guess it's OK to make the attempt to be somewhat creative with how you earn money. For instance, rather than asking your parents for money to buy a pair of Jordans basketball sneakers that cost $250, ask them if you can work to earn $250 so you can buy a pair of sneakers. Then, go buy the cheaper Jordans and save the other $68.24. That's how important saving is. When you engage finances this way—so eager to earn money—that's when you know you are serious about saving.

Once you start working, you should keep working until you are wealthy. If you are planning to be a millionaire by the 2060s, be careful what you wish for, because you may come to realize $1 million will not be worth as much fifty years from now. Any child younger than ten years old should be thinking in bigger and broader terms. By the time the ten-year-old reaches the 2060s, there will be so many trillionaires and billionaires that a millionaire will be like having just $200,000 dollars in the bank. Either way, the time is now to start earning and saving.

For most people, saving money while you attend college will be a challenge. If you are even close to the predicament I found myself in when I decided I was determined to go to college, you will accumulate some level of college-loan debt. On the other hand, if you happen to be a studious person who earns a full scholarship, the rules for you will change, and the opportunity for you to save will be enhanced—but still not easy.

Conversely, if you decide not to make college a priority or a part of your bigger picture plan, you should consider saving $20,000 while working and attending high school. When you're successful, the money could be used to start a mobile nail salon business. Let's look at the math. If you make $15.00 an hour and work twenty hours per week, you will make $300 per week. Assuming you will work for the full year part time, $300 times fifty-two weeks is $15,600 per year. If you work all four years while you're in high school, you will earn $15,600 per year times four years: $62,400. Yep—you could do it. You could pay your taxes, pay your parents $1,200 per year on rent, or have money to buy those Jordans, go on a few dates, and save a minimum of $20,000 to start your first business.

Saving is the foundational basis for building wealth. It's important for every child to start saving as a child; however, it's more important for the child who grows up and lands their first big job to continue saving and, in the process, building wealth. After you graduate from college and you're about to land your ideal job in a Fortune company, be sure to ask about the company's 401K plan or their retirement plan. In addition, you should ask if the company contributes to its employees' retirement plans. Some companies will match your individual contributions to your plan. You may think that at your age (twenty-one or twenty-two, just out of college) it would be too early to start saving money. It's not, and you would be remiss and irresponsible to miss the opportunity to start saving for your future. Company retirement plans are just one way to start saving for your future and your retirement. There are other ways to save if you are not working at a major Fortune company. One of the most popular ways is to open an individual retirement account (IRA). Please check with your bank or a financial advisor to get more information about all the options available to you. Retirement plans are also a good way to delay paying taxes on a portion of your income. This is smart because later in life, when you will be required to pay taxes on that income, you will more than likely pay at a lower tax rate. Finally, the money you contribute to any retirement plan is invested over the years. In the end, when you're ready to retire in the 2060s, your retirement plan may have accumulated to a couple of a million dollars or more. Please don't miss this opportunity to plan.

Tips

- Start saving as a child. Save a portion of your allowance.
- Start working as soon as you are old enough to—be sure to check the federal and state laws.
- Research programs that will allow you to save money for your college education. Like retirement plans, many of these programs will accrue interest, which means when you are ready to use those funds, you will have more money for your education than you deposited over time.
- While in high school, work part time, and save most of the money you make.

- If you know your predicament at your home requires you to contribute to your family, step up and help your mom and dad. God will bless you.
- Always be mindful that there will be children far less fortunate than you; use some of your savings to help others in need.
- Donate to causes like charity and churches.
- Do not waste your money. Saving is far more important than fitting in and showing off.
- As soon as you are eligible, participate in a retirement plan.

The idea of supporting the next generation is paramount. The fact is that children really are our future. When we guide them the right way by instilling within them the right values, making clear the value of them being developed for success, and making clear their obligation to support other children, they will be the ones contributing to the eradication of the plights that plague our country.

18

Efficacy: The 2060s Project Call to Action

The journey to reaching the milestone of this book has been a long and tough one, fraught with ups, downs, and painful truths about my country, my people, my fellow citizens of the United States, and my personal life experiences. Far too many of us seem content with simply living in the now versus owning up to the change we desire and deserve. I've counselled some, with their faded will, to try to do something constructive that might contribute to better life experiences for themselves and their children—today and in the future. "What's the use?" they asked.

At times, I was torn. I even started to question whether I was wasting my time, energy, and money writing a book that tells the truth about our country's dark history, our current state, and my predictions for the future of a nation seemingly content with the status quo. I almost gave in to the naysayers. In the end, I remained grounded in my faith and the realization that this quest is not about me. This directive is out of my control and aligned with God's will. This mission has turned out to be my God-assigned purpose. So, I kept writing. Moreover, I will keep working toward a solution to the cultural plights of the United States.

There are millions of vulnerable children in our country. The targeted demographic is huge—much larger than I can manage on my own. This undertaking will take more than a village. It will take more than a single city. It will take more than a state. In fact, given our country's cultural history, it may take more than the will of the citizenry of our country. For these reasons, I am open to asking any person, group of people, organizations, corporations, city governments, state governments, the US government, and leaders of our country's allies for varying degrees of assistance and support.

Because certain face-to-face interactions with our children will be required, this will not be an easy undertaking. In fact, this book will be of no value unless there is a very serious and purposeful effort connected to it. It is for this reason that I have initiated the 2060s Project.

In the early stages of the 2060s Project, I have been working with a core team of like-minded believers in the plan to reshape the United States' core values. The plan has been to initially take very small steps to lay the foundation for the bigger picture strategy, which will include the complete alteration of cultural values over the next fifty years. It will be a very structured plan, and the children of our country will own most of the change that will happen. However, before our children can fully engage, there must be willing and able adults. Are our citizens ready to take on such a major challenge? Are they at least willing to try? The will of people can be a powerful thing.

On June 23, 1963, Martin Luther King pronounced during a speech in Detroit, Michigan, "If a man has not discovered something he will die for, he isn't fit to live." Almost five years later, on April 4, 1968, Dr. King was assassinated in Memphis, Tennessee, as he was continuing to stand up and fight for the rights and equality of Black American people. While King's view regarding the will of men is firm and, by some accounts, an extreme measure, the question is a valid one. What are we as a people willing to do on this new quest to guide our children through the 2060s with much better life experiences and life outcomes than underserved children have previously had in our country? What are women, children, and men willing to do?

Since the end of slavery, a lot of progress has been made in efforts to equalize the citizenship of Black Americans to the citizenship experience of white Americans. There's clearly more work ahead of us. After King's assassination, there has not been a structured and unified strategy in place with the purpose of addressing systemic discrimination and inequality. On the other side of the equation, the accountability of adults and children related to the intellectual development of our children has been lacking or has fallen short of achieving broad and measurable success. It seems the fight for equality, once so persistent, has all but dissipated after Martin Luther King's assassination. In fact, I will go a step further and suggest there has been willful and unconscientious capitulation.

So here we are. We've come full circle again. However, this time, sitting idly by with inaction is not an option. It's time for Black Americans to lead the way on a broad scale with profound demonstrations. Not the kind of demonstrations symbolized by marches and protests. Black Americans today must start demonstrating the mastery of developing our children for the workforce. They must demonstrate the power of maintaining their personal integrity. Black Americans, including our teens, must demonstrate the relentless will to support the next generation of children so that there will be an assurance that we, too, can legitimately pronounce, "Never again."

Coalescing

I know with absolute certainty that even the thought of bringing US citizens together in support of this paramount cause will be a challenging undertaking. First, we will face the challenge of inspiring and convincing ordinary people of the value of being forward thinkers and planners. Second, the outcomes will not be realized immediately, and in some cases, not for years. Third, it has been made clear that one of the primary reasons this project and strategy are being executed is in support of changing the life trajectory of a group of children whose lives have been and continue to be negatively impacted because of the color of their skin. Generally, our country (our collective citizenry) has not had the appetite to support the Black American community. It's a US reality; however, it is not a broad reality that applies to all the citizens of our country. In this regard, I am hopeful!

I'm hopeful because I know Black Americans will not be deterred. I'm hopeful because we've witnessed a very large faction of white Americans throw support behind meaningful and legitimate causes like the 2060s Project. I'm hopeful because I've witnessed close to one million men travel to and populate Washington, DC, in support of Black American causes—an event I attended back in the 1980s. I'm hopeful because while the United

States is often divided, our country, with its diverse citizenry, delivered a Black American man to the White House as president of the United States. Twice.

The small core group of advocates who are committed to taking the initial agenda forward seem eager to make something happen. Today, I am leading the pack. However, if any of the folks I mentioned in my star power list would even remotely suggest they want to lead, I'd gladly turn the reins over and accept a role in the trenches, leading the way in guiding our children.

The first step in the coalescing process has been to complete this book. It is amazing how authoring a book can somehow legitimize a person and sometimes their agenda or project. I've seen it happen. The 2060s Project can be established on a national scale as a new, legitimate movement.

There is traction already in movement in response to the book being published soon. That traction has come in the form of individual interest, confirmed speaking engagements, and sprinkles of financial support. However, it is important that strict discipline is upheld and all forms of distractions are mitigated. We cannot afford to be preoccupied with lower-hanging fruit and miss opportunities to seize the entire tree. We have fifty years to get this right. Patience will be our strength.

I am completely confident the 2060s Project will attract the appropriate leaders, human resources, and the financial resources required to experience the projected successful outcomes. It's a question of how, when, and at what level. All of which will hinge on our initial leadership's ability to proactively build and leverage a strong efficacy.

In 1982, when Prince dropped the single "1999," everyone seemed to get it. Prince was simply talking about partying today and every day in the future like it was 1999, actually in the future. The song, in some way, represented a prelude to the turn of the new century, and Prince jumped ahead of the game. Ironically, when I wear a cap with the 2060s logo on it or when I'm speaking with people about the 2060s Project, it is not always intuitive that the 2060s is in the future or that my book is about the future. But once they finally get it, the excitement in their faces is genuine and undeniable. Generally, people are aware of the future; however, most people do not think of it or strategically plan for it sufficiently. That's what makes the 2060s Project aberrant. In the end, it will be those excited people from all walks of life that will start thinking and caring about the future and the future of our children.

Our current team is made up mostly of corporate professionals. The core team will continue to grow to a minimum of two hundred advocates in strategic geographies over the next two years. In addition to other roles these advocates might play, each of them will be certified and capable of publicly speaking on the topic of the WIN Model and the value propositions connected to all its seven life principles: reading, education, work, accountability, respect, duty, and saving money.

The next wave of talent will involve bringing on key, prominent leadership figures from different disciplines, such as the corporate world, sports, entertainment, and so on. The goal here will be to continue building the narrative around the 2060s Project and, in the process, solidify its branding. We will exhibit relentless determination to ensure the 2060s movement will become a household name and a topic that will dominate discussions worldwide.

Our primary market is children. Therefore, we will continue to forge relationships with schools, colleges, and universities around the country. The goal of the 2060s Project leadership team is to reach an excess of five million children who will assume the challenge of leading the way by setting examples of what it takes to WIN in the United States. Each of these courageous young men and women will graduate from the WIN Model in full compliance. This will mean they will be completely focused on the following:

- Complete compliance related to their development for the workforce.
- Complete compliance in terms of an assurance that their integrity is consistently intact.
- Compliance in full alignment with ideals for doing all they can to support other children and thereby demonstrate their eagerness and will to ensure the next generation of children will never be left behind again.

Our second market will be parents and adults with influence over children. The goal here is to leverage individuals connected to children on a regular basis for the purpose of echoing positive values and engendering children to focus more seriously on their future. This means making sure young children are being taught to read by age three by any means necessary. I am especially concerned about single mothers, who represent 85 percent of single parents. This is one of the reasons mentoring programs are critically important. Qualified mentors fall into that group of influencers who can make a huge difference in the life of a child living with just his or her mother as the single parent.

We will attend conferences (such as ones for parent-teacher associations, reading, educators, and more) for the purpose of getting our WIN curriculum somehow embedded into schools' curriculums, home engagements around the dinner table, and so on. Imagine if every school taught lessons in the context of workforce development, integrity, and/or the next generation. These fundamental teachings are the ones I missed in my childhood. No child should ever miss out on these basic principles of life in the United States ever again.

Financing

After we lay out a solid business plan, it will be leveraged to inspire the support required to make this grand undertaking a monumental success. There are several potential paths to success. We should start with the simple one—the grassroots approach to prove our persistence.

Looking forward, we have fifty years to go before the 2060s end. In that time, it is possible to raise $50 billion to support this very important and necessary cause via a grassroots campaign. We will ask one million people of all races to make annual donations (once per year) of $1,000. In this model, we will raise $1,000,000,000 per year. Our continued annual success would yield $50 billion by the 2060s. Think about that: $1,000 per year from a single individual or family over the course of a full year is $250 per quarter, or $83.33 per month, or just $2.70 per day. That's a small amount to pay for the sake of saving our children and ensuring they reach the end of the 2060s with enhanced life outcomes. It's a small price to pay to reshape the norms and values of the United States. It's a small price to pay to unite the country once and for all. We can do this.

In addition, we will ask the Gates Foundation, the Buffett Foundation, and any other foundation willing to match our contributions or offer any level of support to drive this agenda forward.

Use of Funds

Given the digital divide in the United States, my initial proposal would be to use the funds to erect mentoring/technology centers in strategic cities around the United States. No basketballs allowed. It's time to work before, during, and after school for the sake of ensuring our children are being guided appropriately and that they get it. That's how dire the concern is for Black American and other underserved children. These centers would be leveraged solely for the purpose of teaching and getting an early start in developing young children for the workforce, especially the information technology workforce.

The funds would cover:

- Capital expenditures and buildout (building) expenditures
- Rent expenses (including buildout)
- Desks
- Supplies
- Human resources—including salaries, corporate tax, health benefits, holiday pay, sick pay, and market value pay increases for instructors, mentors, security, administrative, and janitorial services
- Technology—PCs, cloud services, monitors, network infrastructure, and more
- Utilities—electricity, water, gas
- Landscaping
- Insurance (liability and umbrella, workers' comp, fidelity bonds)
- Training materials
- Technology

I firmly believe that if our children are constantly reminded of their accountability to have WIN Model REWARDS life principles instilled in them, they will start to take the challenge more seriously. Therefore, I am also proposing some of the funds be used for national advertising of the seven REWARDS life principles—including national ads, local ads, super bowl ads, printed ads, and refrigerated magnets. In fact, all types of marketing material should be on the table, including T-shirts, caps, mugs, posters, pens, pencils, bags, hoodies, jackets, and so much more.

I am a member of the Information Technology Senior Management Forum (ITSMF). It's an organization of Black American senior leaders in the IT space. I have had initial discussions with a few executive members from Fortune companies about building a superdata technology to support the 2060s Project. The model would be used to manage and track 100 percent of our young protégés on their journey to the 2060s. I anticipate this talent pool will be in high demand over time as our children are appropriately and intellectually developed. Black American children and others participating in our programs will become prime candidates for high-tech jobs in the United States and the worldwide workforce because their skills will have been perfectly matched and aligned with most of the key highly compensated jobs in the workforce. Major companies will aggressively seek out Black American talent and the talent of other courageous students of the WIN Model who will have finally gotten right what it takes to WIN in our country. These young soldiers will have made contributions to reshaping their personal values and the values of the United States.

I have asked for a lot here. I do so for the sake of an assurance that US children will be positioned to take ownership of their lives as they forge ahead to the 2060s.

Black American people represent some of the absolute best examples of succeeding in the United States. To name a few, think of Michelle Obama, Oprah, the Williams sisters (Venus and Serena), Tiger Woods, Ken Chenault (former CEO at American Express), Michael Jordan, LeBron James, Steph Curry, Clarence Thomas, David L. Steward (chairman of the board at World Wide Technology, Inc.), and Ursula Burns (former CEO at Xerox). There were also notable Black American inventors who paved the way and made possible many of the advances and conveniences the entire world enjoys today. For instance, Mark

E. Dean led the team and made significant contributions to the first personal computer built by IBM; Charles Richard Drew was the doctor responsible for the first major blood bank; Marie Van Brittan Brown invented the first home security system. While the list goes on and I could continue with names for over ten pages, I'd be remiss not to acknowledge Black America's absolute best example of success in the United States of America. I consider this example the best because it wasn't about individual success. This achievement was about the success of people willing to educate themselves and work together. They built buildings and owned companies. They were doctors, lawyers, and entrepreneurs. More importantly, they supported each other and spent the money they earned with other people like them. They built a city just outside of Tulsa, Oklahoma, that because of its success and prominence became known as Black Wall Street. Whatever happened to those days?

Had Black Wall Street survived the attacks by local whites with their guns and gas bombs, the entire Black American community would be entirely different today. Had Black Americans from Black Wall Street mustered up the courage to go back to rebuild their city, their resolve would have made a huge statement that would have resonated across the entire nation. Because it matters in the United States what you're willing to do and where you are willing to do it. Had the Black Wall Street citizens simply moved on to a different US geography, built a new city, and continued to execute their social model for coalescing and their economic development model for winning, there might not be a need for my project.

The town founded, built, and successfully managed by many freed slaves—Black American people—that thrived in the very early 1900s would have represented such an iconic example of Black American success in the United States that the model would have been replicated one thousand times over by now. However, that is not the way the story ended. Consequently, in addition to all the targeted calamity of racism, discrimination, and police brutality, Black American people are still not united as they should or could be. Instead, my call to action is valid, warranted, and needed now more than ever before. I consider this our last stand. Nonetheless, I am hopeful and extraordinarily confident.

My intent was to create a stronger sense of urgency in our adults and children simply to master the most basic and fundamental skills and attributes required to be successful in the United States. This is not rocket science. Furthermore, I have featured the exact same basic lessons most children are taught at varying levels in close to 100 percent of schools and homes around our country. The only thing I have done differently is accentuate the importance of certain skills and attributes, thus advocating for their greater recognition. I was also compelled to articulate in clear terms the consequences of children falling short of effectively honing these skills. In this regard, I believe by creating a different sense of urgency, parents, other adults with influence over children, and children—especially teens— will start immediately taking the childhood experience more seriously and elevate their accountabilities to a higher priority.

Workforce Development

Most of us have witnessed the extraordinary qualities exhibited by children who are well educated and those who know how to keep their integrity in check. The problem is they often seem far and few between. But clearly it is possible to breed these perceived gifted children in greater numbers and at higher levels of quality than the current average.

Any child, regardless of race, color, gender, or sexual orientation, in the United States who is willing to master the concept of intentionally and purposefully developing themselves for specific, highly compensated jobs (such as IT security) in the workforce will find it easier to find work and avoid unemployment and living in poverty. In addition, those courageous individuals willing to develop themselves as entrepreneurs in certain fields such as landscaping, painting, electrical, car detailing, web developing, financial planning, temporary staffing, and so much more will find themselves busy at work with the potential to expand their businesses into multi-million-dollar operations. These capitalists will be setting examples of success, hiring countless people, and raking in the cash.

Conversely, those who fall short of this critical accountability to develop their key skills for the demand of the workforce will struggle to find work despite any headwinds imposed by our culture, such as discrimination. I believe most of our young children will start to take their responsibility to earn money in our country very seriously. As a result, going forward, I project that starting at a minimum of eight years from the time *Own the Change* is published, the unemployment rate for Black Americans will trend downward. There will be measurable increases in students reading at or above their grade levels. Most importantly, illiteracy will start to significantly diminish. College attendance will improve significantly, and graduation rates will spike. More college students will be eager to work in corporate internship programs, and they will land these critically important summer and fall jobs at record rates. I am especially stoked about the increase in the number of young children taking career paths that are today less traveled—fields like the sciences, information technology, engineering, mathematics, and astrophysics.

As these scholars grow older, there will be young children from Birmingham, Alabama, and Jackson, Mississippi, who will rise to the occasion to become doctors, lawyers, and CEOs at major Fortune companies all around the United States. I envision 21 percent of all Fortune company CEOs will be Black American by the start of the 2060s. Notwithstanding the successes of adults of all races who will have made it to the 2060s after instilling the **WIN REWARDS** life principles within them, Black Americans will be showcased as some of the absolute best in class the United States has to offer. Blacks will lead the way in terms of new and futuristic inventions. Included in these masterful inventions might be the first hovering vehicle.

In the end, it will be Black Americans and other US children who will grow up and join forces with other young adults from around the globe to save the world from chronic global warming.

Integrity

Integrity has the power to eliminate the dreadful and divisive norms of our past. The good will embedded within the hearts and souls of people will not allow the same old hateful and polarizing values to prevail. The children will carry the weight of addressing the issues of racism, discrimination, hate, selective privilege, police brutality, mass incarceration, the n-word, and unaccountability. It will be the intrinsic values instilled within our children that will ultimately free our country from the grips of certain ills from our history that still haunt us today.

Far fewer Black American people (per capita) will be incarcerated as our young children will have grown up managing their will to be accountable for the choices they make, thereby avoiding any brushes with the US penal system. In addition, these Black American adults who make it to the 2060s will be sharp and crisp with their language. No, this will not be a matter or question of assimilating or giving in. When Black American people speak English, it will not be perceived by other Black Americans as "sounding white." It will be clearly understood because they will have learned the importance of communicating effectively with people of all races. In this regard, Black Americans will lead the way in learning to speak multiple languages. Black Americans will have forged ahead for the sake of winning with grace and dignity, all while building wealth.

I suspect that one of the most critical success stories that will result from this project will be Black American people learning to support and raise each other up. This is the single variable that could make or break my plan. If Black American people are not willing to come together for the purpose of saving Black American children and the entire race, our failure will be demonstrably self-inflicted. This failure will have absolutely nothing to do with racism or discrimination or any of those kinds of headwinds. Therefore, we cannot allow that to happen. In the end, collective best-in-class Black Americans will trump any and all headwinds or roadblocks put before us. I guarantee it! Just as I guarantee the united Black American family by the 2060s.

Next Generation

Every adult should live their lives free of any doubt about the future of their children and the next generation. By supporting the next generation of children and constantly instilling within our children their God-ordered accountability to do their absolute best, keep their integrity in check and in good standing with no questions about it, and support and guide others who may be weaker or lesser developed, the cycle of winning in the United States will be impenetrable and impossible to break.

For as many years, adults of all races in the United States have fallen short of appropriately equipping our children with the right values required for them to WIN and required for them to have full appreciation of the importance of helping and guiding others—including older children supporting younger ones. This disastrous level of complacency must end. We can no longer leave the success of our children to random chance. We have proven time and time again that when we do, we collectively do them a disservice. Our children deserve better.

So, as we forge ahead, we must do so with purpose and pride. Not just with limited vision and focus on just our personal issues at hand. We have an obligation to leave our past behind and do what's right and necessary to eradicate polarization and to simply do right by the man who envisioned a country "free at last."

The United States will never reach its full capacity if only Black Americans reshape their lives, their vision, and their trajectory. The problem in our country is not just an African American problem. It's much bigger than that. So starting today, and for every day going forward, children of all races must make very conscious choices related to the culture that we will carry forward. It is our job to collectively support these succeeding generations so our country will be an evolved and truly united nation when we reach the 2060s.

Acknowledgments

To Elma Greggs, my aunt—thank you for playing the role of matriarch to our entire family after Mamma left us. She was just sixty-two years old. Your sister, "sis," is looking down on you with a smile and pride in her heart. She's safe and at peace knowing you have kept your promise and her children safe. I see you, Elma. God bless you.

To my entire family, friends, mentors, protégés, associates, and acquaintances, please know that despite our differences, I respect you today and always. This book and the 2060s Project will continue to be more than a notion. Please know that I will unapologetically count on you for help. I will need you on this quest.

John Miller, thank you for taking the time to read my manuscript and write the foreword. I appreciate you. Moreover, I am proud of you, my friend, for your courage and the extraordinary steps you are taking at Denny's Restaurants. I see you! We see you. May God continue guiding and blessing you.

To my friend Bonnie Hearn Hill for your patience, guidance, and support. While I still have work to do, you made me a better writer. You are a blessing!

To Tim O'Brien for the cover illustration.

Ron Parker and Fern Johnson, thanks for your support and for being my sounding boards.

To my very diverse group of friends at 24 Hour Fitness on Preston Road in Frisco, Texas. By now, you know most of what's in the whole book. Thanks for listening.

About the Author

Originally from Birmingham, Alabama, Ralph Harper is a seasoned professional in the information technology industry with a combined thirty-three years of experience, over the course of which he has held several leadership roles at Fortune companies such as Equitable Life, PepsiCo, and Frito-Lay. Throughout his corporate career, Harper has been responsible for proposing, planning, developing, delivering, and supporting enterprise-wide technologies with multi-million-dollar budgets.

Currently, Harper is the president at DPLOYIT Executive Search. Under Harper's leadership, DPLOYIT was recognized by Inc. in 2008 and 2014 as one of the fastest-growing companies in the United States.

Aside from his corporate work, Harper has found his life's purpose in forming strategies to eradicate the generational plight of young, underserved children in the United States by the end of the 2060s. He serves as chairman of the board at Catherine Harper for Keepers (CH4k), a nonprofit organization based in Plano, Texas. CH4k's mission aligns with the initiatives and goals of President Obama's My Brother's Keeper Challenge.

Harper is a motivational speaker who has covered topics relating to business strategies, fatherhood, the plight of underserved children, and what it takes to win in the United States. His speaking venues include Florida Gulf Coast University, the Barack Obama Leadership Academies, the Fatherhood Collaborative in San Mateo County, California, and high schools and job corps campuses around the country. He currently lives in Plano, Texas.